DELIBERATE PRACTICE IN

DIALECTICAL
BEHAVIOR THERAPY

Essentials of Deliberate Practice Series
Tony Rousmaniere and Alexandre Vaz, Series Editors

ESSENTIALS OF DELIBERATE PRACTICE SERIES
TONY ROUSMANIERE AND ALEXANDRE VAZ, SERIES EDITORS

DELIBERATE PRACTICE IN
DIALECTICAL
BEHAVIOR THERAPY

TALI BORITZ

SHELLEY McMAIN

ALEXANDRE VAZ

TONY ROUSMANIERE

 AMERICAN PSYCHOLOGICAL ASSOCIATION

Published by
American Psychological Association
750 First Street, NE
Washington, DC 20002
https://www.apa.org

Order Department
https://www.apa.org/pubs/books
order@apa.org

In the U.K., Europe, Africa, and the Middle East, copies may be ordered from Eurospan
https://www.eurospanbookstore.com/apa
info@eurospangroup.com

Typeset in Cera Pro by Circle Graphics, Inc., Reisterstown, MD

Printer: Gasch Printing, Odenton, MD
Cover Designer: Mark Karis

Library of Congress Cataloging-in-Publication Data

Names: Boritz, Tali, author. | McMain, Shelley, author. | Vaz, Alexandre, author. |
    Rousmaniere, Tony, author.
Title: Deliberate practice in dialectical behavior therapy / Tali Boritz,
    Shelley McMain, Alexandre Vaz, and Tony Rousmaniere.
Description: Washington, DC : American Psychological Association, [2023] |
    Series: Essentials of deliberate practice | Includes bibliographical
    references and index.
Identifiers: LCCN 2022024884 (print) | LCCN 2022024885 (ebook) |
    ISBN 9781433837890 (paperback) | ISBN 9781433837906 (ebook)
Subjects: LCSH: Dialectical behavior therapy. | Psychotherapists--Training
    of. | BISAC: PSYCHOLOGY / Education & Training | PSYCHOLOGY /
    Psychotherapy / General
Classification: LCC RC489.D48 B67 2023 (print) | LCC RC489.D48 (ebook) |
    DDC 616.89/14--dc23/eng/20220716
LC record available at https://lccn.loc.gov/2022024884
LC ebook record available at https://lccn.loc.gov/2022024885

https://doi.org/10.1037/0000322-000

Printed in the United States of America

10 9 8 7 6 5 4 3 2 1

We dedicate this book to Marsha Linehan, who pioneered research in the field of personality disorders and emotion dysregulation and the development of dialectical behavior therapy. We are truly grateful to Marsha for what she has achieved for the field of mental health. Her brilliant therapy has changed lives across the world, touching thousands of people, families, health care professionals, and others impacted by borderline personality disorder and other mental health problems related to emotion dysregulation.

Contents

Series Preface

Tony Rousmaniere and Alexandre Vaz

We are pleased to introduce the Essentials of Deliberate Practice series of training books. We are developing this book series to address a specific need that we see in many psychology training programs. The issue can be illustrated by the training experiences of Mary, a hypothetical second-year graduate school trainee. Mary has learned a lot about mental health theory, research, and psychotherapy techniques. Mary is a dedicated student; she has read dozens of textbooks, written excellent papers about psychotherapy, and receives near-perfect scores on her course exams. However, when Mary sits with her clients at her practicum site, she often has trouble performing the therapy skills that she can write and talk about so clearly. Furthermore, Mary has noticed herself getting anxious when her clients express strong reactions, such as getting very emotional, hopeless, or skeptical about therapy. Sometimes this anxiety is strong enough to make Mary freeze at key moments, limiting her ability to help those clients.

During her weekly individual and group supervision, Mary's supervisor gives her advice informed by empirically supported therapies and common factor methods. The supervisor often supplements that advice by leading Mary through role-plays, recommending additional reading, or providing examples from her own work with clients. Mary, a dedicated supervisee who shares tapes of her sessions with her supervisor, is open about her challenges, carefully writes down her supervisor's advice, and reads the suggested readings. However, when Mary sits back down with her clients, she often finds that her new knowledge seems to have flown out of her head, and she is unable to enact her supervisor's advice. Mary finds this problem to be particularly acute with the clients who are emotionally evocative.

Mary's supervisor, who has received formal training in supervision, uses supervisory best practices, including the use of video to review supervisees' work. She would rate Mary's overall competence level as consistent with expectations for a trainee at Mary's developmental level. But even though Mary's overall progress is positive, she experiences some recurring problems in her work. This is true even though the supervisor is confident that she and Mary have identified the changes that Mary should make in her work.

The problem with which Mary and her supervisor are wrestling—the disconnect between her knowledge about psychotherapy and her ability to reliably perform psychotherapy—is the focus of this book series. We started this series because most therapists experience this disconnect, to one degree or another, whether they are beginning trainees or highly experienced clinicians. In truth, we are all Mary.

To address this problem, we are focusing this series on the use of deliberate practice, a method of training specifically designed for improving reliable performance of complex skills in challenging work environments (Rousmaniere, 2016, 2019; Rousmaniere et al., 2017). Deliberate practice entails experiential, repeated training with a particular skill until it becomes automatic. In the context of psychotherapy, this involves two trainees role-playing as a client and a therapist, switching roles every so often, under the guidance of a supervisor. The trainee playing the therapist reacts to client statements, ranging in difficulty from beginner to intermediate to advanced, with improvised responses that reflect fundamental therapeutic skills.

To create these books, we approached leading trainers and researchers of major therapy models with these simple instructions: Identify 10 to 12 essential skills for your therapy model where trainees often experience a disconnect between cognitive knowledge and performance ability—in other words, skills that trainees could write a good paper about but often have challenges performing, especially with challenging clients. We then collaborated with the authors to create deliberate practice exercises specifically designed to improve reliable performance of these skills and overall responsive treatment (Hatcher, 2015; Stiles et al., 1998; Stiles & Horvath, 2017). Finally, we rigorously tested these exercises with trainees and trainers at multiple sites around the world and refined them based on extensive feedback.

Each book in this series focuses on a specific therapy model, but readers will notice that most exercises in these books touch on common factor variables and facilitative interpersonal skills that researchers have identified as having the most impact on client outcome, such as empathy, verbal fluency, emotional expression, persuasiveness, and problem focus (e.g., Anderson et al., 2009; Norcross et al., 2019). Thus, the exercises in every book should help with a broad range of clients. Despite the specific theoretical model(s) from which therapists work, most therapists place a strong emphasis on pantheoretical elements of the therapeutic relationship, many of which have robust empirical support as correlates or mechanisms of client improvement (e.g., Norcross et al., 2019). We also recognize that therapy models have already-established training programs with rich histories, so we present deliberate practice not as a replacement but as an adaptable, transtheoretical training method that can be integrated into these existing programs to improve skill retention and help ensure basic competency.

About This Book

This book in the series is on dialectical behavior therapy (DBT), an integrative behavioral treatment used to treat individuals with severe emotional and behavioral dysregulation, such as borderline personality disorder. DBT training typically involves learning the theories that underlie the DBT model, observing expert practice, experiential exercises (e.g., role-playing), supervised clinical work, and participation on a DBT consultation team. Deliberate practice is intended as an additional piece designed to enhance DBT training. It is not intended to be the only delivery format through which DBT skills are acquired, nor is this book sufficient on its own for obtaining full proficiency in DBT. However, the practice of the skills set forth in this book provides trainees with the opportunity to translate their didactic learning of DBT to a simulated environment that mimics the clinical interaction, which can later be applied with actual clients. This book provides opportunities for trainees to experiment using DBT skills with a range of client presentations and clinical scenarios; to practice what they would say and how they would say it. We hope this book stimulates your interest and engagement in DBT and supports your ongoing development as DBT therapists in training!

Acknowledgments

We would like to acknowledge Rodney Goodyear for his significant contribution to starting and organizing this book series. We are grateful to Susan Reynolds, David Becker, Elizabeth Budd, Emily Ekle, and Joe Albrecht at American Psychological Association (APA) Books for providing expert guidance and insightful editing that has significantly improved the quality and accessibility of this book. We also acknowledge the International Deliberate Practice Society (IDPS) and its members for their many contributions and support for our work. Finally, we are grateful for the invaluable editorial notes and feedback from Inês Amaro, Amy DeSmidt, and Jamie Manser.

The exercises in this book underwent extensive testing at training programs around the world. For all the pilot site leaders and trainees who volunteered to "test run" this work and provided critically important feedback, we cannot thank you enough. We are deeply grateful to the following supervisors and trainees, who tested exercises and/or provided invaluable feedback:

- Herbert Assaloni and Mirjam Tanner, private practice, Winterthur, Switzerland
- Paul Bizzotto, private practice, Albury, New South Wales, Australia
- Jen Davies-Owen, Breathe Therapies, Liverpool, England, United Kingdom
- Konstadina Griva, Nanyang Technological University, Singapore
- Anna-Maija Kokko, Center for Cognitive Psychotherapy Luote Ltd, Mikkeli, Finland
- Natasha Kostek, private practice, New York, NY, United States
- Kerry-Jayne Lambert and Adam Digby, University of Roehampton, London, England, United Kingdom
- Crystal Morrissey, Yorkville University, Fredericton, New Brunswick, Canada
- Selina Phan, Ferkauf School of Psychology, New York, NY, United States
- Hugo Pedro Sousa, private practice, Lisboa, Portugal
- Margot Stafford, Regis University, Denver, CO, United States
- Catarina Telo, private practice, London, England, United Kingdom
- Lianna Trubowitz, Ferkauf Graduate School of Psychology, New York, NY, United States
- Alix Velasco, The Welsh Psychotherapy Institute, Cardiff, Wales, United Kingdom
- Yi Yang and Jane E. Keat, private practice, Boston, MA, United States

Overview and Instructions

In Part I, we provide an overview of deliberate practice, including how it can be integrated into clinical training programs for dialectical behavior therapy (DBT), and instructions for performing the deliberate practice exercises in Part II. **We encourage both trainers and trainees to read both Chapters 1 and 2 before performing the deliberate practice exercises for the first time.**

Chapter 1 provides a foundation for the rest of the book by introducing important concepts related to deliberate practice and its role in psychotherapy training more broadly and DBT training more specifically. We review three broad categories of DBT strategies: acceptance-focused strategies, change-focused strategies, and dialectical strategies. We also individually review the 12 skills included in the deliberate practice exercises.

Chapter 2 lays out the basic, most essential instructions for performing the DBT deliberate practice exercises in Part II. They are designed to be quick and simple and provide you with just enough information to get started without being overwhelmed by too much information. Chapter 3 in Part III provides more in-depth guidance, which we encourage you to read once you are comfortable with the basic instructions in Chapter 2.

Introduction and Overview of Deliberate Practice and Dialectical Behavior Therapy

Dialectical behavior therapy (DBT) is an evidence-based psychotherapy typically used to treat individuals with severe emotional and behavioral dysregulation, such as borderline personality disorder (BPD). Learning DBT can be a daunting task. DBT is a comprehensive behavioral treatment that includes numerous therapeutic strategies and techniques that are dialectically balanced between accepting the client as they are within a context of trying to teach them how to change (i.e., use more effective coping strategies). As a principle-driven therapy, the effective delivery of DBT requires therapists to have a strong grasp of the foundational theories underlying the treatment. When paired with an individualized DBT case formulation based on frequent and thorough behavioral assessment, these principles serve as guidelines for the application of DBT strategies and techniques.

Adding to the treatment complexity is the client population for whom DBT was originally designed: severe, high-risk individuals with pervasive difficulties regulating emotion. Treating complex clients can be challenging, even for the most seasoned therapists. When clients are emotionally dysregulated or present with high-risk behaviors, therapists are especially vulnerable to becoming reactive (e.g., becoming overly accommodating or overly rigid in their practice). Therefore, a large part of DBT training and skill development involves learning how to flexibly respond to clients across a range of clinical scenarios.

This book is designed to facilitate the acquisition of foundational DBT skills. Through deliberate practice, these DBT skills will eventually become more fluid and natural and will help trainees respond effectively and flexibly in their work with complex clients. The exercises included in this book are aimed at developing DBT skills in response to a diverse set of clinical presentations and situations.

https://doi.org/10.1037/0000322-001

Deliberate Practice in Dialectical Behavior Therapy, by T. Boritz, S. McMain, A. Vaz, and T. Rousmaniere

Overview of the Deliberate Practice Exercises

The main focus of the book is a series of exercises that have been thoroughly tested and modified based on feedback from trainees and DBT clinicians and trainers. The first 12 exercises each represent an essential DBT strategy or skill. The last two exercises are more comprehensive, consisting of an annotated DBT transcript and improvised mock therapy sessions that teach practitioners how to integrate all these skills into more expansive clinical scenarios. Table 1.1 presents the 12 skills that are covered in these exercises.

Throughout all the exercises, trainees work in pairs under the guidance of a supervisor and role-play as a client and a therapist, switching back and forth between the two roles. Each of the 12 skill-focused exercises consists of multiple client statements grouped by difficulty—beginner, intermediate, and advanced—that call for a specific skill. For each skill, trainees are asked to read through and absorb the description of the skill, its criteria, and some examples of it. The trainee playing the client then reads the statements, which portray a range of possible problems and emotional states typically seen in clients presenting for DBT. The trainee playing the therapist then responds in a way that demonstrates the specified DBT skill. Trainee therapists will have the option of practicing a response using the one supplied in the exercise or immediately improvising and supplying their own.

After each client statement and therapist response couplet is practiced several times, the trainees will stop to receive feedback from the supervisor. Guided by the supervisor, the trainees will be instructed to try statement–response couplets several times, working their way down the list. In consultation with the supervisor, trainees will go through the exercises, starting with the least challenging and moving through to more advanced levels. The triad (supervisor–client–therapist) will have the opportunity to discuss whether exercises present too much or too little challenge and adjust up or down depending on the assessment.

Trainees, in consultation with supervisors, can decide which skills they wish to work on and for how long. On the basis of our testing experience, we have found practice sessions last about 1 to 1.25 hours to receive maximum benefit. After this, trainees become saturated and need a break.

Ideally, learners will both gain confidence and achieve competence by practicing these exercises. Competence is defined here as the ability to perform a specific DBT strategy or skill in a manner that is flexible and responsive to the client. Skills have been chosen that are considered essential to DBT and that practitioners often find challenging to implement.

TABLE 1.1. The 12 Dialectical Behavior Therapy Skills Presented in the Deliberate Practice Exercises

Beginner Skills	Intermediate Skills	Advanced Skills
1. Establishing a session agenda 2. Validation 3. Reinforcing adaptive behaviors 4. Problem assessment	5. Eliciting a commitment 6. Inviting the client to engage in problem solving 7. Skills training 8. Modifying cognitions 9. Informal exposure to emotions	10. Coaching clients in distress 11. Promoting dialectical thinking through both–and statements 12. Responding to suicidal ideation

The skills identified in this book are not comprehensive in the sense of representing all one needs to learn to become a competent DBT clinician. Some will present particular challenges for trainees. A short history of DBT and a brief description of the deliberate practice methodology is provided to explain how we have arrived at the union between them.

The Goals of This Book

The primary goal of this book is to help trainees acquire and develop core DBT skills. Therefore, the expression of that skill or competency may look somewhat different across clients or even within a session with the same client.

The DBT deliberate practice exercises are designed to achieve the following:

1. Help learners develop the ability to apply the skills in a range of clinical situations.

2. Move the DBT strategies and skills into procedural memory (Squire, 2004) so that learners can access them even when they are overwhelmed, stressed, or discouraged.

3. Provide learners with an opportunity to practice the DBT strategy or skill using a style and language that is congruent with who they are.

4. Provide the opportunity to use the DBT strategy or skill in response to varying client statements and affect. This is designed to build confidence to adopt skills in a broad range of circumstances within different client contexts.

5. Provide DBT learners with many opportunities to fail and then correct their failed response based on feedback. This helps build confidence and persistence.

Finally, this book aims to help trainees discover their own personal learning style so that they can continue their professional development long after their formal training is concluded.

Who Can Benefit From This Book?

This book is designed to be used in multiple contexts, including in graduate-level courses, supervision, postgraduate training, and continuing education programs. It assumes the following:

1. The trainer is knowledgeable about and competent in DBT.

2. The trainer can provide good demonstrations of how to use DBT strategies and skills across a range of therapeutic situations, via role-play and/or video. Or the trainer has access to examples of DBT being demonstrated through the many psychotherapy video examples available (see McMain & Wiebe, 2013; Tullos et al., 2014; Yalom et al., 2013).

3. The trainer can provide feedback to students regarding how to craft or improve their application of DBT strategies and skills.

4. Trainees will have accompanying reading, such as books and articles, that explain the theory, research, and rationale of DBT and each particular strategy and skill. Recommended reading for each skill is provided in the sample syllabus (Appendix C).

The exercises covered in this book were piloted in 15 training sites from across four continents (North America, Europe, Asia, and Oceania). The book is designed for trainers and trainees from different cultural backgrounds worldwide.

This book is also designed for those who are training at all career stages, from beginning trainees, including those who have never worked with real clients, to seasoned therapists. All exercises feature guidance for assessing the adjusting of the difficulty to precisely target the needs of each individual learner. The term "trainee" in this book is used broadly, referring to anyone in the field of professional mental health who is endeavoring to acquire skills in the DBT. For further guidance on how to improve multicultural deliberate practice skills, see the forthcoming book *Deliberate Practice in Multicultural Therapy* (Harris et al., 2022).

Deliberate Practice in Psychotherapy Training

How does one become an expert in their professional field? What is trainable, and what is simply beyond our reach due to innate or uncontrollable factors? Questions such as these touch on our fascination with expert performers and their development. A mixture of awe, admiration, and even confusion surround people such as Mozart, da Vinci, or more contemporary top performers such as basketball legend Michael Jordan and chess virtuoso Garry Kasparov. What accounts for their consistently superior professional results? Evidence suggests that the amount of time spent on a particular type of training is a key factor in developing expertise in virtually all domains (Ericsson & Pool, 2016). *Deliberate practice* is an evidence-based method that can improve performance in an effective and reliable manner.

The concept of deliberate practice has its origins in a classic study by K. Anders Ericsson and colleagues (1993). They found that the amount of time practicing a skill and the quality of the time spent doing so were key factors predicting mastery and acquisition. They identified five key activities in learning and mastering skills: (a) observing one's own work, (b) getting expert feedback, (c) setting small incremental learning goals just beyond the performer's ability, (d) engaging in repetitive behavioral rehearsal of specific skills, and (e) continuously assessing performance. Ericsson and his colleagues termed this process deliberate practice, a cyclical process that is illustrated in Figure 1.1.

Research has shown that lengthy engagement in deliberate practice is associated with expert performance across a variety of professional fields, such as medicine, sports, music, chess, computer programming, and mathematics (Ericsson et al., 2018). People may associate deliberate practice with the widely known "10,000-hour rule" popularized by Malcolm Gladwell in his 2008 book, *Outliers*, although the actual number of hours required for expertise varies by field and by individual (Ericsson & Pool, 2016). This, however, perpetuated two misunderstandings. The first is that this is the number of deliberate practice hours that everyone needs to attain expertise, no matter the domain. In fact, there can be considerable variability in how many hours are required.

The second misunderstanding is that engagement in 10,000 hours of work performance will lead one to become an expert in that domain. This misunderstanding holds considerable significance for the field of psychotherapy, where hours of work experience with clients has traditionally been used as a measure of proficiency (Rousmaniere, 2016). Research suggests that the amount of experience alone does not predict therapist

FIGURE 1.1. Cycle of Deliberate Practice

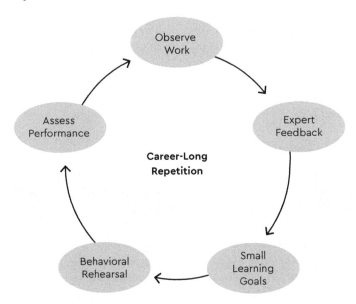

Note. Reprinted from *Deliberate Practice in Emotion-Focused Therapy* (p. 7), by R. N. Goldman, A. Vaz, and T. Rousmaniere, 2021, American Psychological Association (https://doi.org/10.1037/0000227–000). Copyright 2021 by the American Psychological Association.

effectiveness (Goldberg et al., 2016). It may be that the *quality* of deliberate practice is a key factor.

Psychotherapy scholars, recognizing the value of deliberate practice in other fields, have recently called for deliberate practice to be incorporated into training for mental health professionals (e.g., Bailey & Ogles, 2019; Hill et al., 2020; Rousmaniere et al., 2017; Taylor & Neimeyer, 2017; Tracey et al., 2015). There are, however, good reasons to question analogies made between psychotherapy and other professional fields, like sports or music, because by comparison psychotherapy is so complex and free form. Sports have clearly defined goals, and classical music follows a written score. In contrast, the goals of psychotherapy shift with the unique presentation of each client at each session. Therapists do not have the luxury of following a score.

Instead, good psychotherapy is more like improvisational jazz (Noa Kageyama, as cited in Rousmaniere, 2016). In jazz improvisations, a complex mixture of group collaboration, creativity, and interaction is coconstructed among band members. Like psychotherapy, no two jazz improvisations are identical. However, improvisations are not a random collection of notes. They are grounded in a comprehensive theoretical understanding and technical proficiency that is only developed through continuous deliberate practice. For example, prominent jazz instructor Jerry Coker (1990) listed 18 skill areas that students must master, each of which has multiple discrete skills including tone quality, intervals, chord arpeggios, scales, patterns, and licks. In this sense, more creative and artful improvisations are actually a reflection of a previous commitment to repetitive skill practice and acquisition. As legendary jazz musician Miles Davis put it, "You have to play a long time to be able to play like yourself" (Cook, 2005, p. 112).

The main idea that we stress here is that we want deliberate practice to help therapists learning DBT to feel comfortable bringing their unique personalities and styles into their practice. The idea is to learn the skills so that you have them on hand when you want them. Practice the skills to make them your own. Incorporate those aspects that feel right for you. Ongoing and effortful deliberate practice should not be an impediment to flexibility and creativity. Ideally, it should enhance it. We recognize and celebrate that psychotherapy is an ever-shifting encounter and by no means want it to become or feel formulaic. Competent DBT therapists are able to use DBT skills adeptly while ensuring responsiveness to the individual client and their context. The core DBT responses provided are meant as templates or possibilities, rather than "answers." Please interpret and apply them as you see fit, in a way that makes sense to you. We encourage flexible and improvisational play!

Simulation-Based Mastery Learning

Deliberate practice uses simulation-based mastery learning (Ericsson, 2004; McGaghie et al., 2014). That is, the stimulus material for training consists of "contrived social situations that mimic problems, events, or conditions that arise in professional encounters" (McGaghie et al., 2014, p. 375). A key component of this approach is that the stimuli being used in training are sufficiently similar to the real-world experiences, so that they mimic that they provoke similar reactions. This facilitates *state-dependent learning*, in which professionals acquire skills in the same psychological environment where they will have to perform the skills (Fisher & Craik, 1977). For example, pilots train with flight simulators that present mechanical failures and dangerous weather conditions, and surgeons practice with surgical simulators that present medical complications. Training in simulations with challenging stimuli increases professionals' capacity to perform effectively under stress. For the psychotherapy training exercises in this book, the "simulators" are typical client statements that might be presented in the course of therapy sessions and call upon the use of the particular skill.

Declarative Versus Procedural Knowledge

Declarative knowledge is what a person can understand, write, or speak about. It often refers to factual information that can be consciously recalled through memory and often acquired relatively quickly. In contrast, procedural learning is implicit in memory and "usually requires *repetition of an activity*, and associated learning is demonstrated through *improved task performance*" (Koziol & Budding, 2012, pp. 2694, emphasis added). *Procedural knowledge* is what a person can perform, especially under stress (Squire, 2004). There can be a wide difference between their declarative and procedural knowledge. For example, an "armchair quarterback" is a person who understands and talks about athletics well but would have trouble performing it with a professional ability. Likewise, most dance, music, or theater critics have a very high ability to write about their subjects but would be flummoxed if asked to perform them.

In DBT training, the gap between declarative and procedural knowledge appears when a trainee or therapist can recognize and appreciate—for example, the need for a validating response that helps the client feel understood when emotionally aroused but has trouble providing effective validation with real clients even when they want to in a given moment. **The sweet spot for deliberate practice is the gap between declarative and procedural knowledge.** In other words, effortful practice should target those skills that the trainee could write a good paper about but would have trouble actually performing with a real client. We start with declarative knowledge, learning skills theoretically and observing others perform them. Once skills are learned, with the help of deliberate practice, we work toward the development of procedural learning, with the aim of therapists having "automatic" access to each of the skills that they can pull on when necessary.

Let us turn to a little theoretical background on DBT to help contextualize the skills of the book and how they fit into the greater training model.

DBT: Theoretical Overview

The theoretical foundation of DBT integrates learning theory, Zen Buddhism, and dialectical philosophy. *Learning theory* states that all behavior is learned and that behavioral change occurs via the principles of learning. This is addressed through the DBT change strategies, which include an emphasis on problem solving. *Zen Buddhism* contends that suffering increases with attachment to things being a particular way and decreases with the acceptance of reality and its limitations. This is addressed through the DBT acceptance strategies, which include an emphasis on validation. At the core of treatment is *dialectical philosophy*, which emphasizes the value of searching for and finding syntheses between natural tensions to bring about change. In DBT, the central dialectic involves striking a balance between change and acceptance; clients are encouraged, on one hand, to acknowledge and accept emotional experience and, on the other, to use a variety of strategies and skills to bring about behavioral change.

DBT conceptualizes pervasive emotion dysregulation as the core dysfunction underlying BPD and other clinical disorders associated with severe emotion dysregulation problems (e.g., substance use, eating disorders). *Emotion dysregulation* refers to difficulty effectively modulating and expressing emotion across a range of contexts. In its extreme form, such as in the case of BPD, emotion dysregulation is pervasive, occurring with frequency and intensity across many contexts. From a DBT perspective, dysfunction across multiple domains of functioning (cognitive, behavioral, interpersonal, self/identity) is an inevitable consequence of dysregulated emotions, or maladaptive attempts to cope with intense and distressing emotion (Linehan, 1993a, 1993b).

DBT's *biosocial theory* posits that pervasive emotion dysregulation results from a transaction between an individual's biological predisposition toward emotional vulnerability and an invalidating environment that minimizes, ignores, or punishes emotion expression and communicates to a person that their understanding of events and internal experiences is wrong. Over time, this transaction leads to problems with emotion regulation, including difficulties understanding, labeling, tolerating, and modulating emotional responses; effectively communicating emotional needs; and effectively solving the problems contributing to emotional distress (Linehan, 1993a, 1993b). Problematic behaviors, including extreme behaviors such as self-harm, suicide attempts, and substance use, are seen as attempts to regulate emotion, or as the result of failed attempts to regulate emotion. Over time, these behaviors become reinforced as avoidance or escape behaviors from aversive emotional states.

While learning any new therapy approach can be a daunting task, even for the brightest of students, it can be especially challenging for trainees learning DBT because the therapy typically involves treating clients who are highly sensitive, reactive, and impulsive. We have found this to be a little like learning under fire as our clients can be unpredictable, and, more importantly, high risk behaviors can arise quickly. DBT trainees are often required to adapt quickly to challenging clinical situations. This requires an ability to simultaneously modulate one's own emotional reactions while fluidly employing a range of diverse treatment skills and techniques to appropriately respond to the client and clinical context. DBT addresses these challenges by articulating a set of principles therapists use to guide clinical decision making. These principles are designed to enhance therapist effectiveness and adherence to the treatment model while remaining flexible and responsive to the client. DBT therapists flexibly apply treatment principles within a highly structured and comprehensive treatment program, typically delivered via four modes of intervention: individual therapy, skills training group, between-session phone coaching, and a consultation team for therapists.

In DBT, all treatment strategies directly or indirectly aim to decrease emotion dysregulation and associated maladaptive responses, and to enhance emotion regulation and adaptive responses. Treatment strategies in DBT are dialectically balanced between accepting the client as they are within a context of trying to teach them how to change (i.e., use more effective coping strategies). Key DBT strategies include (a) acceptance strategies focused on the adoption of a nonjudgmental therapeutic stance and the use of validation (i.e., explicit communications about what makes sense about a client's responses), (b) change strategies focused on problem assessment and problem solving, and (c) dialectical strategies focused on balancing acceptance and change-focused strategies to address polarization and promote synthesis between opposing positions. Most of the DBT skills embody a dialectical approach; this is reflected in the skills criteria for the exercises in this book, most of which include both acceptance- and change-focused responses.

The Role of Deliberate Practice in DBT Training

Returning to the metaphor described earlier in this chapter, the practice of DBT—like deliberate practice more broadly—has a lot in common with playing jazz. Similar to jazz musicians, it is important for DBT therapists to be able to improvise and respond in an agile and creative manner to rapidly evolving and sometimes unpredictable contexts. Developing competence as a DBT therapist requires foundational knowledge in DBT theory and a solid understanding of the principles underlying the treatment strategies, as these form the basis on which a clinical decision to intervene one way or another is made.

Similar to other therapies, beginning training in DBT typically starts with didactic learning, such as through reading treatment manuals and attending seminars and workshops to develop a foundational theoretical understanding of the DBT model. As training progresses, trainees begin practicing DBT with actual clients and focus shifts to skill development both in the delivery of DBT techniques and in case formulation, and feedback is provided via supervision or consultations as well as through direct observation of therapy sessions. At all stages of training, there is a strong emphasis on experiential practice. For example, trainees are expected to participate in role-plays, practice DBT skills themselves, engage in mindfulness practice, and complete homework exercises.

Neither this book nor the deliberate practice method in general is intended to be sufficient for obtaining competence in DBT on its own. The skills included in this book are ideally embedded in a practicum course (see the sample syllabus in Appendix C). Trainees should have prior or parallel exposure to DBT theory and application in dedicated coursework and readings. In line with what we said earlier in this chapter, this loosely reflects the distinction between declarative and procedural knowledge. The DBT deliberate practice methods outlined in this book are not intended to be a primary source of declarative knowledge or to replace or replicate work with actual clients or training cases and case-based supervision (e.g., with review of actual session audio or video). Nevertheless, we envision this book as being useful for DBT training and professional development at all levels. Deliberate practice methods can play a complementary role in DBT training, in the service of augmenting core readings and work performance with real clients. With this in mind, in Appendix C, we recommend resources that provide more information about DBT principles, skills, and training for trainees at all stages of development. Deliberate practice methods provide the first opportunity for a trainee to translate their didactic learning of DBT to a simulated environment that mimics the clinical interaction, which can later be applied with actual clients.

DBT Skills in Deliberate Practice

We have thus far provided a brief introduction to DBT and highlighted how deliberate practice methods are particularly well-suited to the DBT paradigm. In the following sections, we describe the categorization of different DBT skills and outline the skills that will be the focus of the deliberate practice exercises in this book. In addition, we address the importance of the therapeutic relationship in DBT.

Categorizing DBT Skills

We endeavored to distinguish among (a) beginner foundational/structural DBT skills, (b) intermediate-level DBT strategies, and (c) advanced DBT strategies. With this in mind, we considered (a) establishing a session agenda, (b) validation, (c) reinforcing adaptive behavior, and (d) problem assessment to be foundational/structural skills. In turn, we considered (a) eliciting a commitment, (b) inviting the client to engage in problem solving, (c) modifying cognitions, (d) informal emotional exposure, and (e) skills training to be intermediate DBT skills. Finally, we considered (a) promoting dialectical thinking through both–and statements, (b) coaching clients in distress, and (c) responding to suicidal ideation to be advanced DBT strategies.

The DBT Skills Presented in Exercises 1 Through 12

The exercises in this text use a developmentally informed pedagogy in which more advanced skills build on less advanced skills, as indicated in Table 1.1. The beginner level exercises consist of the most basic DBT skills used in most sessions. Establishing a session agenda (Exercise 1) is an essential element for structuring therapy time and prioritizing a session focus. Problems are prioritized according to the degree to which they impede the client's quality of life: Therapy tasks focused on life-threatening behavior take precedence over behaviors that interfere with the therapy itself, which take precedence over other maladaptive behaviors that are interfering with the client's well-being. Validation (Exercise 2) is a core acceptance strategy that communicates to a client that their responses make sense and are understandable in some way. Valida-tion also involves a nonjudgmental therapeutic stance in which the therapist engages with the client in a genuine and authentic manner, treating the client as equal and capable and with respect. Reinforcement of adaptive behaviors (Exercise 3) is used to strengthen adaptive behaviors, including gradual approximations toward behaviors the client is trying to increase. Problem assessment (Exercise 4) is a core change strategy that focuses on understanding the functional relationship between a behavior and its antecedents and consequences.

The first of the intermediate exercises focuses on eliciting a commitment (Exercise 5), which occurs when a therapist seeks explicit agreement from the client to work on mutu-ally determined goals or engage in specific therapy tasks. Problem solving (Exercise 6) involves helping the client identify maladaptive responses or problem behaviors with more skillful and effective responses. Problem solving includes generating, evaluating, and implementing solutions for identified problems. One of these solutions may be skills training (Exercise 7), which is used when the client has a deficit of coping skills and therefore needs support from the therapist to acquire and practice specific effective behaviors. Another solution involves modifying cognitions (Exercise 8) to help the client enhance their ability to observe and identify maladaptive thinking and its impacts, and then to work towards changing or replacing cognitive errors or biases with more adaptive and dialectical thinking. Informal emotional exposure (Exercise 9) is a solution used to address emotional avoidance. Informal exposure involves helping clients understand the principles of exposure and the adaptive function of emotions, focusing the client on their emotions in the here and now, and encouraging them to experience their emotions without escape or avoidance.

The advanced exercises are placed at the end because they require a deeper understanding of DBT theory and principles and involve more complex skills for managing higher risk client behaviors. All the skills in the advanced section build on the earlier skills. Coaching clients in distress (Exercise 10) involves assisting clients in crisis or moments of extreme emotional distress to effectively use skills to down regulate intense emotion. Promoting dialectical thinking through both-and statements (Exercise 11) weaves together validation and change strategies to help clients shift polarized or extreme responses to more balanced, effective responses. Finally, responding to suicidal ideations (Exercise 12) involves assessing and highlighting the emotional problem driving the client's thoughts of escape or avoidance and helping the client consider more effective ways to solve the emotional problem driving their suicidal thoughts.

A Note About Managing Self-Harm and Suicidal Behaviors in DBT

DBT was originally developed as a treatment for people at chronic risk of suicide (Linehan, 1993a, 1993b) and has been most extensively applied with adults with borderline personality disorder engaging in self-harm and suicidal behaviors (Cristea et al., 2017; Stoffers et al., 2012; Storebø et al., 2020). Although a growing literature has now established DBT's efficacy for a wide range of problems, many clients referred for DBT engage in extreme behaviors associated with emotion dysregulation, including suicidal thoughts, gestures, and actions. For this reason, we have provided client statements referencing self-harm and suicidal ideation across all exercises that can help DBT learners develop skills for responding more effectively when presented with these issues in a therapy session.

It is important to note that these exercises alone are insufficient for competently responding to and managing suicide risk. How a therapist responds to any single instance of a self-harm and suicidal behavior should always be guided by and informed by the client's risk history, their current context and situation, a personalized case formulation that includes an understanding of the function of self-harm and suicidal behaviors for the client, and the therapeutic relationship. **At all stages of training, supervision and consultation should be sought when determining how best to respond and intervene if your client expresses suicidal ideation or discloses self-harm or suicidal behavior.**

For additional resources on managing suicide risk in DBT, supervisors and learners may wish to familiarize themselves with the Linehan risk assessment and management protocol (LRAMP; Linehan, 2016). The LRAMP is an empirically supported framework that is commonly used in DBT for assessing, managing, and documenting suicide risk. It also provides a guide to support clinical decision-making as therapists consider various options for intervening with suicidal clients.

The Therapeutic Relationship in DBT

A strong therapeutic relationship is central to DBT and is the primary vehicle for engaging clients in treatment and increasing motivation and willingness to change (Linehan, 1993a, 1993b). DBT therapists strive to engage with their clients with warmth, compassion, and acceptance. Additionally, DBT therapists are encouraged to be fully present to the client and the unfolding therapy process, including being awake to subtle shifts in the client in-session or in the therapist's own reactions or behaviors toward the client. Adopting an open, curious, and nonjudgmental stance can help therapists remain balanced and less reactive in the face of challenging situations. This promotes trust in the relationship and engagement in therapy, which in turn allows the client to be open to emotional experiencing and expression as well as new learning experiences and problem solving. These qualities are conveyed both verbally (e.g., through the use of validation) and also through nonverbal and paralinguistic cues, such as vocal quality, tone, and posture. For further discussion of the therapeutic relationship in DBT, learners may wish to review additional writing, such as Bedics et al. (2012a, 2012b, 2015), Boritz et al. (2023), Rizvi (2011), and Shearin and Linehan (1992).

Overview of the Book's Structure

This book is organized into three parts. Part I contains this chapter and Chapter 2, which provides basic instructions on how to perform these exercises. We found through testing that providing too many instructions upfront overwhelmed trainers and trainees, and they skipped past them as a result. Therefore, we kept these instructions as brief and simple as possible to focus only on the most essential information that trainers and trainees will need to get started with the exercises. Further guidelines for getting the most out of deliberate practice are provided in Chapter 3, and additional instructions for monitoring and adjusting the difficulty of the exercises are provided in Appendix A. **Do not skip the instructions in Chapter 2, and be sure to read the additional guidelines and instructions in Chapter 3 and Appendix A once you are comfortable with the basic instructions.**

Part II contains the 12 skill-focused exercises, which are ordered based on their difficulty: beginner, intermediate, and advanced (see Table 1.1). They each contain a brief overview of the exercise, example client–therapist interactions to help guide trainees, step-by-step instructions for conducting that exercise, and a list of criteria for mastering the relevant skill. The client statements and sample therapist responses are then presented, also organized by difficulty (beginner, intermediate, and advanced). The statements and responses are presented separately so that the trainee playing the therapist has more freedom to improvise responses without being influenced by the sample responses, which should only be turned to if the trainee has difficulty improvising their own responses. The last two exercises in Part II provide opportunities to practice the 12 skills within simulated psychotherapy sessions. Exercise 13 provides a sample psychotherapy session transcript in which the DBT skills are used and clearly labeled, thereby demonstrating how they might flow together in an actual therapy session. DBT trainees are invited to run through the sample transcript with one playing the therapist and the other playing the client to get a feel for how a session might unfold. Exercise 14 provides suggestions for undertaking mock sessions, as well as client profiles ordered by difficulty (beginner, intermediate, and advanced) that trainees can use for improvised role-plays.

Part III contains Chapter 3, which provides additional guidance for trainers and trainees. While Chapter 2 is more procedural, Chapter 3 covers big-picture issues. It highlights six key points for getting the most out of deliberate practice and describes the importance of appropriate responsiveness, attending to trainee well-being and respecting their privacy, and trainer self-evaluation, among other topics.

Three appendixes conclude this book. Appendix A provides instructions for monitoring and adjusting the difficulty of each exercise as needed. It provides a Deliberate Practice Reaction Form for the trainee playing the therapist to complete to indicate whether the exercise is too easy or too difficult. Appendix B includes a Deliberate Practice Diary Form that can be used to during a training session's final evaluation to process the trainees' experiences, but its primary purpose is to provide trainees a format to explore and record their experiences while engaging in additional, between-session deliberate practice activities without the supervisor. Appendix C presents a sample syllabus demonstrating how the 12 deliberate practice exercises and other support material can be integrated into a more comprehensive DBT training course. Instructors may choose to modify the syllabus or pick elements of it to integrate into their own courses.

Downloadable versions of this book's appendixes, including a color version of the Deliberate Practice Reaction Form, can be found in the "Clinician and Practitioner Resources" tab at https://www.apa.org/pubs/books/deliberate-practice-dialectical-behavior-therapy.

Instructions for the Dialectical Behavior Therapy Deliberate Practice Exercises

This chapter provides basic instructions that are common to all the exercises in this book. More specific instructions are provided in each exercise. Chapter 3 also provides important guidance for trainees and trainers that will help them get the most out of deliberate practice. Appendix A offers additional instructions for monitoring and adjusting the difficulty of the exercises as needed after getting through all then client statements in a single difficulty level, including a Deliberate Practice Reaction Form the trainee playing the therapist can complete to indicate whether they found the statements too easy or too difficult. **Difficulty assessment is an important part of the deliberate practice process and should not be skipped.**

Overview

The deliberate practice exercises in this book involve role-plays of hypothetical situations in therapy. The role-play involves three people: one trainee role-plays the therapist, another trainee role-plays the client, and a trainer (professor/supervisor) observes and provides feedback. Alternatively, a peer can observe and provide feedback.

This book provides a script for every role-play, each with a client statement and an example therapist response. The client statements are graded in difficulty from beginning to advanced, although these difficulty grades are only estimates. The actual perceived difficulty of client statements is subjective and varies widely by trainee. For example, some trainees may experience a stimulus of a client being angry to be easy to respond to, whereas another trainee may experience it as very difficult. Thus, it is important for trainees to provide difficulty assessments and adjustments to ensure that they are practicing at the right difficulty level: neither too easy nor too hard.

https://doi.org/10.1037/0000322-002
Deliberate Practice in Dialectical Behavior Therapy, by T. Boritz, S. McMain, A. Vaz, and T. Rousmaniere

Time Frame

We recommend a 90-minute time block for every exercise, structured roughly as follows:

- First 20 minutes: Orientation. The trainer explains the dialectical behavior therapy (DBT) skill and demonstrates the exercise procedure with a volunteer trainee.

- Middle 50 minutes: Trainees perform the exercise in pairs. The trainer or a peer provides feedback throughout this process and monitors/adjusts the exercise's difficulty as needed after each set of statements (see Appendix A for more information about difficulty assessment).

- Final 20 minutes: Review, feedback, and discussion.

Preparation

1. Every trainee will need their own copy of this book.

2. Each exercise requires the trainer to fill out a Deliberate Practice Reaction Form after completing all the statements from a single difficulty level. This form is available in the "Clinician and Practitioner Resources" tab at https://www.apa.org/pubs/books/deliberate-practice-dialectical-behavior-therapy and in Appendix A.

3. Trainees are grouped into pairs. One volunteers to role-play the therapist and one to role-play the client (they will switch roles after 15 minutes of practice). As noted previously, an observer who might be either the trainer or a fellow trainee will work with each pair.

The Role of the Trainer

The primary responsibilities of the trainer are as follows:

1. Provide corrective feedback, which includes both information about how well the trainees' response met expected criteria and any necessary guidance about how to improve the response.

2. Remind trainees to do difficulty assessments and adjustments after each level of client statements is completed (beginning, intermediate, and advanced).

How to Practice

Each exercise includes its own step-by-step instructions. Trainees should follow these instructions carefully, as every step is important.

Skill Criteria

Each of the 12 exercises focuses on one essential DBT strategy or skill with one to three skill criteria that describe the important components or principles for that skill.

The goal of the role-play is for trainees to practice improvising responses to the client statement in a manner that (a) is attuned to the client, (b) meets skill criteria as much as possible, and (c) feels authentic for the trainee. Trainees are provided scripts with example therapist responses to give them a sense of how to incorporate the skill criteria into a response. **It is important, however, that trainees do not read the example responses verbatim in the role-plays!** Therapy is highly personal and improvisational; the goal of deliberate practice is to develop trainees' ability to improvise within a consistent framework. Memorizing scripted responses would be counterproductive for helping trainees learn to perform therapy that is responsive, authentic, and attuned to each individual client.

Tali Boritz and Shelley McMain wrote the scripted example responses; however, trainees' personal style of therapy may differ slightly or greatly from that in the example scripts. It is essential that, over time, trainees develop their own style and voice, while simultaneously being able to intervene according to the model's principles and strategies. To facilitate this, the exercises in this book were designed to maximize opportunities for improvisational responses informed by the skill criteria and ongoing feedback. For example, in "Modifying Cognitions" (Exercise 8), scripted example responses were designed to focus more on cognitions. In "Informal Exposure to Emotions" (Exercise 9), scripted example responses were designed to focus more on emotions. However, for each of the client statements in these skills exercises, there might be a range of appropriate therapist responses using skills developed in other exercises. Similarly, in an actual therapy session, there may be several equally effective ways a DBT therapist can respond to their client. While working your way through the skills exercises, it can be helpful to consider both how to practice a specific skill and the alternative skills you could potentially use to respond to each client statement. In this way, there's a unique opportunity to strengthen the use of specific skills, while developing flexibility and responsiveness.

Review, Feedback, and Discussion

The review and feedback sequence after each role-play has these two elements:

- First, the trainee who played the client **briefly** shares how it felt to be on the receiving end of the therapist's response. This can help assess how well trainees are attuning with the client.

- Second, the trainer provides **brief** feedback (less than 1 minute) based on the skill criteria for each exercise. Keep feedback specific, behavioral, and brief to preserve time for skill rehearsal. If one trainer is teaching multiple pairs of trainees, the trainer walks around the room, observing the pairs and offering brief feedback. When the trainer is not available, the trainee playing the client gives peer feedback to the therapist, based on the skill criteria and how it felt to be on the receiving end of the intervention. Alternatively, a third trainee can observe and provide feedback.

Trainers (or peers) should remember to keep all feedback specific and brief and not to veer into discussions of theory. There are many other settings for extended discussion of DBT theory and research. In deliberate practice, it is of utmost importance to maximize time for continuous behavioral rehearsal via role-plays.

Final Evaluation

After both trainees have role-played the client and the therapist, the trainer provides an evaluation. Participants should engage in a short group discussion based on this evaluation. This discussion can provide ideas for where to focus homework and future deliberate practice sessions. To this end, Appendix B presents a Deliberate Practice Diary Form, which can also be downloaded from the "Clinician and Practitioner Resources" tab at https://www.apa.org/pubs/books/deliberate-practice-dialectical-behavior-therapy. This form can be used as part of the final evaluation to help trainees process their experiences from that session with the supervisor. However, it is designed primarily to be used by trainees as a template for exploring and recording their thoughts and experiences between sessions, particularly when pursuing additional deliberate practice activities without the supervisor, such as rehearsing responses alone or if two trainees want to practice the exercises together—perhaps with a third trainee filling the supervisor's role. Then, if they want, the trainees can discuss these experiences with the supervisor at the beginning of the next training session.

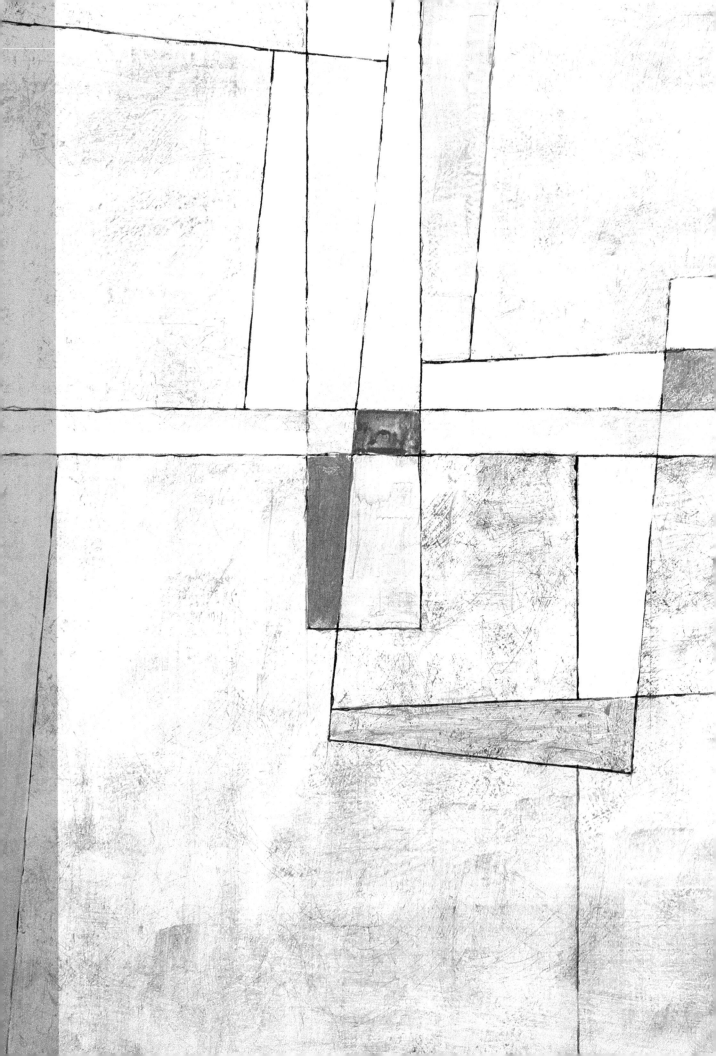

Deliberate Practice Exercises for Dialectical Behavior Therapy Skills

This section of the book provides 12 deliberate practice exercises for essential dialectical behavior therapy (DBT) skills. These exercises are organized in a developmental sequence, from those that are more appropriate to someone just beginning DBT training to those intended for individuals who have progressed to a more advanced level. Although we anticipate that most trainers would use these exercises in the order we have suggested, some may find it more appropriate to their training circumstances to use a different order. We also provide two comprehensive exercises that bring together the DBT skills using an annotated DBT session transcript and mock DBT sessions.

Establishing a Session Agenda

Preparations for Exercise 1

1. Read the instructions in Chapter 2.

2. Download the Deliberate Practice Reaction Form and Deliberate Practice Diary Form at https://www.apa.org/pubs/books/deliberate-practice-dialectical-behavior-therapy (see the "Clinician and Practitioner Resources" tab; also available in Appendixes A and B, respectively).

Skill Description

Skill Difficulty Level: Beginner

Establishing a session focus is an essential element in structuring a dialectical behavior therapy (DBT) session. It is not uncommon for clients to present to a session in an emotionally dysregulated state, reporting many complex problems that need attention. By bringing structure to the session, therapists can help the session feel less chaotic and overwhelming for both themselves and their clients, which can decrease emotional arousal and increase focus and clarity. In DBT, therapy sessions begin by collaboratively setting a session agenda to establish a session focus. Determining the focus of a specific individual therapy session begins with assessing the presence or absence of previously agreed-upon target behaviors (i.e., specific behaviors the client wants to increase or decrease) in the preceding week. This task is typically accomplished by reviewing the client's weekly DBT diary card, which tracks all relevant behaviors during the past week.

Because there may be multiple target behaviors that have occurred since the previous session, the DBT treatment hierarchy is used to prioritize how session time will be spent. Highest priority treatment targets are suicidal and life-threatening behaviors (e.g., suicide attempts, self-harm, suicidal ideation and suicidal communications). The second

https://doi.org/10.1037/0000322-003

highest priority behaviors are therapy-interfering behaviors, which refer to any client or therapist behavior that impedes the client's progress in treatment or compromises the therapy relationship (e.g., attendance issues, not completing homework, lack of collaboration). The third highest priority are behaviors that interfere significantly with the client's quality of life (e.g., substance use, relationship issues, housing). Although more than one target behavior is frequently addressed in a therapy session, when time is tight or a problem is complex, the higher priority target takes precedence (Linehan, 1993a, 1993b). Clients are oriented to the treatment hierarchy in the pretreatment phase of DBT.

Although setting an agenda and establishing a treatment focus help to organize the session, this process is done in collaboration with the client; their input should be directly solicited, and the agenda should be based on values-driven goals they are motivated to work toward. When using this skill, the therapist should maintain a stance of curiosity, openness, flexibility, and acceptance.

SKILL CRITERIA FOR EXERCISE 1

1. The therapist puts forward ideas for a session agenda based on DBT's target hierarchy:
   i. Suicidal and life-threatening behaviors (e.g., suicide attempts, self-harm, suicidal ideation, and suicidal communications).
   ii. Therapy-interfering behaviors (e.g., attendance issues, not completing homework, lack of collaboration).
   iii. Quality of life-interfering behaviors (e.g., substance use, relationship issues, housing).
2. The therapist invites the client's input on the session agenda.

Examples of Establishing a Session Agenda

Example 1

CLIENT: [*Crying*] I had the worst week. I got in a big fight with my boyfriend and ended up self-harming.

THERAPIST: Sounds like a really hard week. I'd like to hear more about what led to the self-harm. (Criterion 1) But let me check in with you—what would you like to put on the agenda for today? (Criterion 2)

Example 2

CLIENT: [*Neutral*] I don't really have anything to talk about this week. Nothing happened. I spent most of the week just avoiding everything.

THERAPIST: Maybe we can put that on the agenda? I'd like to hear more about what you were avoiding and why. (Criterion 1) How does that sound? (Criterion 2)

Example 3

CLIENT: [*Shame*] I didn't do my homework. Every time I tried to do it, I felt overwhelmed.

THERAPIST: It's so great you tried to do it. I wonder if it would be helpful to spend some time talking about what happened when you tried to do the homework? (Criterion 1) I'm also curious what you would like to focus on today? (Criterion 2)

INSTRUCTIONS FOR EXERCISE 1
Step 1: Role-Play and Feedback
• The client says the first beginner client statement. The therapist improvises a response based on the skill criteria. • The trainer (or, if not available, the client) provides brief feedback based on the skill criteria. • The client then repeats the same statement, and the therapist again improvises a response. The trainer (or client) again provides brief feedback.
Step 2: Repeat
• Repeat Step 1 for all the statements at the current difficulty level (beginner, intermediate, or advanced).
Step 3: Assess and Adjust Difficulty
• The therapist completes the Deliberate Practice Reaction Form (see Appendix A) and decides whether to make the exercise easier, harder, or to repeat the same difficulty level.
Step 4: Repeat for Approximately 15 Minutes
• Repeat Steps 1 to 3 for at least 15 minutes. • The trainees then switch therapist and client roles and start over.

> **Now it's your turn! Follow Steps 1 and 2 from the instructions.**

Remember: The goal of the role-play is for trainees to practice improvising responses to the client statements in a manner that (a) uses the skill criteria and (b) feels authentic for the trainee. **Example therapist responses for each client statement are provided at the end of this exercise. Trainees should attempt to improvise their own responses before reading the example responses.**

BEGINNER-LEVEL CLIENT STATEMENTS FOR EXERCISE 1
Beginner Client Statement 1
[Sad] This has been an awful week. I felt on the verge of a panic attack the whole week and missed a bunch of deadlines for school.
Beginner Client Statement 2
[Tired] Sorry I'm 30 minutes late to today's session. I came running and almost didn't make it at all.
Beginner Client Statement 3
[Proud] I didn't have any drinks last week. I didn't self-harm either. . . . Well, I started to cut myself once but stopped pretty quickly.
Beginner Client Statement 4
[Irritated] I used a lot of skills this week. I mean, I needed to—my parents were driving me crazy, I got into a fight with my sister because she took their side, and then when I tried to call you for help you didn't answer your phone.
Beginner Client Statement 5
[Neutral] With the weather getting warmer, I want to wear T-shirts, but I'm embarrassed about my old scars. I've been cutting on my leg instead, where I can hide them better. But I don't really want to talk about that. What I really want to talk about is how to handle this situation with my boss at work.

 Assess and adjust the difficulty before moving to the next difficulty level (see Step 3 in the exercise instructions).

INTERMEDIATE-LEVEL CLIENT STATEMENTS FOR EXERCISE 1
Intermediate Client Statement 1
[Shame] I don't really know where to start. I feel like I can't do anything right. I missed group this week because I was so overwhelmed. I almost didn't come today because I'm so stressed out.
Intermediate Client Statement 2
[Neutral] There's a lot I want to talk about it today. I need help figuring out how to talk to my partner about their anger. They really lose their temper over little things, and it's stressing me out. Yesterday they yelled at me because I forgot to pick up groceries. But I was so depressed. I could barely get off the couch. They just don't get how hard things are for me right now.
Intermediate Client Statement 3
[Happy] I have some news. I just got offered a job, but it's during the day so I won't be able to come here anymore.
Intermediate Client Statement 4
[Neutral] I don't have a preference on what we talk about today. You can decide.
Intermediate Client Statement 5
[Sad] It doesn't matter what we talk about today. Nothing is changing.

 Assess and adjust the difficulty before moving to the next difficulty level (see Step 3 in the exercise instructions).

ADVANCED-LEVEL CLIENT STATEMENTS FOR EXERCISE 1
Advanced Client Statement 1
[Irritated] I'm not sure what you want me to say. My week was fine. It's this therapy that's the problem. I come here for help, but every week I leave feeling worse.
Advanced Client Statement 2
[Sad] It was a difficult week. I'm not sure if I can talk about it.
Advanced Client Statement 3
[Excited] I did the homework, and it went really well. I tried the DEAR MAN skill on my girlfriend yesterday, and it totally diffused a fight. The night before, we got into a huge argument and I hit myself, which made everything worse. But yesterday, I was more regulated, and we talked it out.
Advanced Client Statement 4
[Shame] I tried using skills, but I felt suicidal all week. I tried to distract myself, but the thoughts kept coming. It's just too much. I can't live like this.
Advanced Client Statement 5
[Neutral] My mom wants me to talk to you today about sleep. She thinks I sleep too much and that it's something we should be focusing on in therapy.

> ✋ **Assess and adjust the difficulty here (see Step 3 in the exercise instructions). If appropriate, follow the instructions to make the exercise even more challenging (see Appendix A).**

Example Therapist Responses: Establishing a Session Agenda

Remember: Trainees should attempt to improvise their own responses before reading the example responses. **Do not read the following responses verbatim unless you are having trouble coming up with your own responses!**

EXAMPLE RESPONSES TO BEGINNER-LEVEL CLIENT STATEMENTS FOR EXERCISE 1
Example Response to Beginner Client Statement 1
That's too bad. I wonder if it would be helpful for us to spend some time talking about what was going on this week that made you feel so anxious. (Criterion 1) What do you think about that? What would you like us to focus on today? (Criterion 2)
Example Response to Beginner Client Statement 2
I'm glad you made it. Given we don't have too much time today, what's on your agenda for today? (Criterion 2) One thing I'm thinking is that we should talk about how to get you in on time for our sessions! (Criterion 1) It's important we figure this out together.
Example Response to Beginner Client Statement 3
I'd love to hear more about how you abstained for a full week. Let's make sure we spend some time on this so we can figure out what helped you be so effective. Perhaps we can start though by talking a bit about the cutting. I'm curious to hear more about what happened that led up to the cutting, and also how you stopped yourself. (Criterion 1) How does that plan sound to you? (Criterion 2)
Example Response to Beginner Client Statement 4
It sounds like there was a lot going on this week. I'm glad you used skills, but I'm also hearing that you tried to reach out for support and I wasn't there. That sounds frustrating and disappointing, and I'd really like to put that on the top of the agenda and talk more about it. (Criterion 1) What do you think? Is there anything else you want to make sure we get to today? (Criterion 2)
Example Response to Beginner Client Statement 5
OK—both of those sound really important! It sounds like your situation with your boss is top of your mind right now, and I think it's important we talk about the cutting you've been doing on your legs. Let's figure out a way to address both of these today. (Criterion 1) Does that sound OK to you? (Criterion 2)

EXAMPLE RESPONSES TO INTERMEDIATE-LEVEL CLIENT STATEMENTS FOR EXERCISE 1

Example Response to Intermediate Client Statement 1

It sounds like there are a few things we could focus on today. It sounds like you're feeling overwhelmed and stressed out, and that's getting in the way of making it into therapy. That seems like a priority. It would be great to figure out together how to help you with that overwhelmed feeling and to come up with a solid plan for making it into group or individual therapy even if you're feeling overwhelmed. (Criterion 1) What do you think? (Criterion 2)

Example Response to Intermediate Client Statement 2

That does sound like a lot. Let's start by figuring out our priorities for today's session. You've mentioned you want to talk about communicating effectively to your partner. You also mentioned feeling pretty depressed. (Criterion 1) Where would you like to start today? And is there anything else you haven't mentioned yet but want to make sure we put on the agenda? (Criterion 2)

Example Response to Intermediate Client Statement 3

That's great news about the job. I'd love to understand more about your thoughts on ending therapy. Sounds like this should be a priority focus for our session today. (Criterion 1) Does that make sense to you? Is there anything else you were hoping to talk about today? (Criterion 2)

Example Response to Intermediate Client Statement 4

Why don't we look at your diary card and figure out what to focus on? (Criterion 1) We can look it over together and see which priorities may be the most important for today. (Criterion 2)

Example Response to Intermediate Client Statement 5

It sounds like you're feeling pretty hopeless today. I wonder if that would be a good place to start? (Criterion 1) What do you think about that? (Criterion 2)

EXAMPLE RESPONSES TO ADVANCED-LEVEL
CLIENT STATEMENTS FOR EXERCISE 1

Example Response to Advanced Client Statement 1

This is super important. I'd like to understand more about what's happening in our therapy that's leaving you feeling so badly after our sessions. I would suggest we put this at the top of the agenda. (Criterion 1) What do you think? Does this seem like a reasonable place to focus our time today, or are there other things you want to make sure we cover? (Criterion 2)

Example Response to Advanced Client Statement 2

I'd really like to hear more about what made this such a difficult week. (Criterion 1) Are you willing to put that on the agenda, even if it's hard to talk about? (Criterion 2)

Example Response to Advanced Client Statement 3

I'm glad the homework went well! I'm also hearing that before trying the homework, there was a fight that involved you hitting yourself. It would probably make sense to talk both about what happened with hitting and also how you turned things around with skills the next day. Perhaps we can focus first on the self-harm and then on the skills? (Criterion 1) Does that order make sense to you? (Criterion 2)

Example Response to Advanced Client Statement 4

Seems like it would make sense to put managing suicidal thoughts on the agenda. (Criterion 1) It sounds like you tried to use some skills, but it wasn't quite enough this week. Let's see if we can do some problem solving together. How does that sound to you as a focus for our session? (Criterion 2)

Example Response to Advanced Client Statement 5

It's helpful to hear your mom's concerns. We can definitely put sleep on the agenda if it's something you want to talk about. (Criterion 1) Is sleep something you want to talk about today? Is there anything else you want to make sure we focus on? (Criterion 2)

Validation

Preparations for Exercise 2

1. Read the instructions in Chapter 2.

2. Download the Deliberate Practice Reaction Form and Deliberate Practice Diary Form
   at https://www.apa.org/pubs/books/deliberate-practice-dialectical-behavior-therapy
   (see the "Clinician and Practitioner Resources" tab; also available in Appendixes A
   and B, respectively).

Skill Description

Skill Difficulty Level: Beginner

Validation is the core acceptance strategy in dialectical behavior therapy (DBT). Validation
is used to communicate acceptance and to help clients understand that their responses
make sense and are understandable in some way. When people feel invalidated (e.g.,
when we are told our descriptions or understandings of our internal experiences are
wrong, or our responses are due to undesirable or unacceptable character traits), it is
common for emotional arousal to increase. Many DBT clients have a history of pervasive
invalidation and are emotionally vulnerable; as a result, they may be particularly sensitive to invalidation both outside of and within therapy sessions. A heightened state of
emotional arousal can interfere with information processing, new learning, and problem
solving—necessary requirements for therapeutic change. Validation is therefore essential in DBT for multiple reasons: It (a) decreases emotional arousal, (b) helps clients learn
to trust their responses, (c) makes problem solving possible, and (d) strengthens the
therapeutic alliance.

Validation is conveyed both through a general therapeutic stance and as a set of
communication strategies. A validating therapeutic stance involves engaging with the
client in a genuine and nonjudgmental manner. Validation is also an explicit communication

https://doi.org/10.1037/0000322-004
Deliberate Practice in Dialectical Behavior Therapy, by T. Boritz, S. McMain, A. Vaz, and T. Rousmaniere

regarding what makes sense about the client's thoughts, feelings, or actions. Validation can be communicated by accurately reflecting or summarizing the client's expressed thoughts, emotions, and urges ("You felt really angry when your friend cancelled plans"); it also includes articulations of those aspects of the client's internal experience that are unverbalized ("It sounds like in addition to feeling angry at your friend, you were also feeling quite hurt"). Validation can also be communicated by contextualizing the client's responses given their past learning, history, biology, and cognitive style or by identifying what makes sense about their responses in light of their current situation or normative responding.

It is essential that therapists only validate what makes sense about the client's response and avoid validating the invalid. For example, a client may respond to a nagging parent by yelling and screaming at them until they back off. In this case, the therapist could validate that many people might find a nagging parent irritating and the desire to want to end an unpleasant encounter is understandable, while highlighting that yelling and screaming may not be the most effective way to solve the problem.

SKILL CRITERIA FOR EXERCISE 2

1. The therapist accurately reflects the client's explicit or unexpressed thoughts, feelings, or actions.
2. The therapist conveys what is understandable or makes sense about the client's thoughts, feelings, or actions.

COMMON MISTAKES

1. The therapist interacts in an overly professional manner or fragilizes the client.
2. The therapist reinforces the client with praise instead of validation.
3. The therapist is misattuned to the client (e.g., doesn't understand the essence of the client's response).
4. The therapist validates the invalid (i.e., aspects of the client's response that are ineffective or incompatible with their long-term goals).

Examples of Validation

Example 1

CLIENT: [*Frustrated*] You're not listening to me. This is hard! I just want to leave this session.

THERAPIST: I can see how frustrated you are. (Criterion 1) It makes sense you might want to leave, if you are feeling like I'm not listening to you or helping you solve your problem. (Criterion 2)

> **Common Therapist Mistake 1:** The therapist fragilizes the client: I'm so sorry I made you feel that way. It makes sense you want to leave the session.

Example 2

CLIENT: [*Sad*] I don't have any friends. I have nobody. I'm just going to kill myself.

THERAPIST: Wow, it sounds like you're feeling really alone and hopeless. (Criterion 1) I can understand how your thoughts might go to killing yourself if you think that's the only way to get relief from your misery. (Criterion 2)

> **Common Therapist Mistake 2:** The therapist reinforces the client with praise instead of using validation: It's so great you're sharing that with me! It must have been so hard to tell me that.

Example 3

CLIENT: [*Ashamed*] I didn't complete my diary card. You're probably pissed I forgot again.

THERAPIST: You look like you're feeling a lot of shame right now. (Criterion 1) I can imagine feeling pretty upset if I thought my therapist was going to be mad at me. (Criterion 2)

> **Common Therapist Mistake 3:** The therapist is misattuned to the client (e.g., doesn't understand the essence of what is being communicated): It can be really difficult to complete the diary card. Sounds like you're feeling pretty disappointed in yourself.

Example 4

CLIENT: [*Angry*] My mom just wouldn't stop nagging me. I asked her to leave me alone, but she just kept going. So I got really in her face and screamed at her. I think I scared her. Whatever. She backed off.

THERAPIST: It sounds like your emotions were getting pretty intense in that situation and you were looking for a way to end the situation. I can totally understand feeling irritated or overwhelmed and wanting to stop whatever is setting off those feelings. (Criterion 1) It sounds like in that way, your screaming at your mom helped solve that problem in the short term. (Criterion 2)

> **Common Therapist Mistake 4:** The therapist validates the invalid: You were so angry. It makes sense you lost control and screamed at her. Anyone might have that response if they were in that situation.

INSTRUCTIONS FOR EXERCISE 2

Step 1: Role-Play and Feedback

- The client says the first beginner client statement. The therapist improvises a response based on the skill criteria.
- The trainer (or, if not available, the client) provides brief feedback based on the skill criteria.
- The client then repeats the same statement, and the therapist again improvises a response. The trainer (or client) again provides brief feedback.

Step 2: Repeat

- Repeat Step 1 for all the statements at the current difficulty level (beginner, intermediate, or advanced).

Step 3: Assess and Adjust Difficulty

- The therapist completes the Deliberate Practice Reaction Form (see Appendix A) and decides whether to make the exercise easier or harder or to repeat the same difficulty level.

Step 4: Repeat for Approximately 15 Minutes

- Repeat Steps 1 to 3 for at least 15 minutes.
- The trainees then switch therapist and client roles and start over.

> Now it's your turn! Follow Steps 1 and 2 from the instructions.

Remember: The goal of the role-play is for trainees to practice improvising responses to the client statements in a manner that (a) uses the skill criteria and (b) feels authentic for the trainee. **Example therapist responses for each client statement are provided at the end of this exercise. Trainees should attempt to improvise their own responses before reading the example responses.**

BEGINNER-LEVEL CLIENT STATEMENTS FOR EXERCISE 2
Beginner Client Statement 1
[Sad; looking at the floor and not making eye contact] I'm feeling so depressed today and wasn't even planning on coming to our session.
Beginner Client Statement 2
[Frustrated] No one understands how hard it is for me. I try really hard and nothing ever changes.
Beginner Client Statement 3
[Angry] I want to quit group. I feel like they're all judging me.
Beginner Client Statement 4
[Neutral] I was on my way to the liquor store but just as I was about to go in, I saw my boss and turned around. I felt so embarrassed. He thinks I'm in recovery.
Beginner Client Statement 5
[Sad] Nobody cares about me. Nobody is doing anything to help me.

 Assess and adjust the difficulty before moving to the next difficulty level (see Step 3 in the exercise instructions).

INTERMEDIATE-LEVEL CLIENT STATEMENTS FOR EXERCISE 2
Intermediate Client Statement 1
[Crying] I'm such a burden; everyone would be better off without me.
Intermediate Client Statement 2
[Frustrated] You don't get it—I'd use skills if I could, but when I get anxious, I go from zero to 100. There's no time to use skills!
Intermediate Client Statement 3
[Sad] The only friend I have doesn't want to have anything to do with me and now I have nobody.
Intermediate Client Statement 4
[Neutral] When I smoke weed, it just calms my brain down—I find it soothing, and it helps me feel normal.
Intermediate Client Statement 5
[Defensive] Yeah, I lost my temper at him, but he deserved it. It was his fault for getting me so angry in the first place.

🛑 **Assess and adjust the difficulty before moving to the next difficulty level (see Step 3 in the exercise instructions).**

ADVANCED-LEVEL CLIENT STATEMENTS FOR EXERCISE 2
Advanced Client Statement 1
[Angry] This is bullshit. I told you what the problem is, and you just don't want to help me.
Advanced Client Statement 2
[Withdrawn; looking down and not making eye contact] I don't know what to say.
Advanced Client Statement 3
[Crying and hyperventilating] I can't deal with this anymore. I'm done trying.
Advanced Client Statement 4
[Frustrated] I'm angry at myself because I'm a coward. I want to kill myself, but I'm just too afraid.
Advanced Client Statement 5
[Angry] You're just like the rest of them. You're going to fire me too, aren't you?

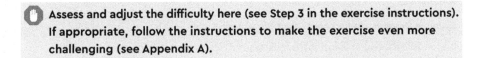 **Assess and adjust the difficulty here (see Step 3 in the exercise instructions). If appropriate, follow the instructions to make the exercise even more challenging (see Appendix A).**

Example Therapist Responses: Validation

Remember: Trainees should attempt to improvise their own responses before reading the example responses. **Do not read the following responses verbatim unless you are having trouble coming up with your own responses!**

EXAMPLE RESPONSES TO BEGINNER-LEVEL CLIENT STATEMENTS FOR EXERCISE 2
Example Response to Beginner Client Statement 1
Sounds like it's been a really challenging day! (Criterion 1) It can be hard to find the energy or motivation to do hard work when you're feeling low. (Criterion 2)
Example Response to Beginner Client Statement 2
It makes sense you're feeling frustrated. (Criterion 1) You're working really hard, and it can feel pretty discouraging when changes aren't happening as quickly as you'd like. (Criterion 2)
Example Response to Beginner Client Statement 3
It sounds like being in the group is feeling pretty uncomfortable for you. (Criterion 1) If I thought everyone was judging me, I'd also have a hard time staying in a group. (Criterion 2)
Example Response to Beginner Client Statement 4
It sounds like seeing your boss brought up a lot of shame. (Criterion 1) I wouldn't want anyone seeing me doing something that I already feel guilty or ashamed about. (Criterion 2)
Example Response to Beginner Client Statement 5
It sounds like you feel like you've been abandoned right now. (Criterion 1) I think most people would feel sad and frustrated if they thought nobody cared about them and they couldn't get the help they needed. (Criterion 2)

EXAMPLE RESPONSES TO INTERMEDIATE-LEVEL CLIENT STATEMENTS FOR EXERCISE 2

Example Response to Intermediate Client Statement 1

You feel like the people you care about would have an easier time if you weren't around. (Criterion 1) If I was thinking everyone was experiencing me as a burden, I'd feel pretty badly too and want to pull away. (Criterion 2)

Example Response to Intermediate Client Statement 2

I wonder if I'm coming off as judgmental or like I'm minimizing just how hard it is to use skills when you're distressed. (Criterion 1) When emotions are really intense, it can really feel like there's not a second to think, let alone stop and use a skill. (Criterion 2)

Example Response to Intermediate Client Statement 3

That sounds so painful. (Criterion 1) I think anyone thinking they were alone in the world would be feeling the way you are right now. (Criterion 2)

Example Response to Intermediate Client Statement 4

It sounds like there are times you feel not so great and are looking for a way to change how you're feeling. (Criterion 1) It makes sense to me that you would want to smoke weed if it helps you feel better. (Criterion 2)

Example Response to Intermediate Client Statement 5

It sounds like he did something that really upset you. (Criterion 1) Anger is a normal response when people do things to us that we don't like. (Criterion 2)

EXAMPLE RESPONSES TO ADVANCED-LEVEL CLIENT STATEMENTS FOR EXERCISE 2
Example Response to Advanced Client Statement 1
You're feeling pretty frustrated with me, huh? (Criterion 1) It's really hard to be in so much distress and to feel like no one's listening or trying to help. (Criterion 2)
Example Response to Advanced Client Statement 2
It looks like you're having a hard time speaking with me right now. (Criterion 1) When emotions are this intense, it's normal to have difficulty knowing what to say or do. (Criterion 2)
Example Response to Advanced Client Statement 3
You're in so much pain. (Criterion 1) It's normal to want to end the feeling of pain. It sounds like you're feeling tired of trying so hard. (Criterion 2)
Example Response to Advanced Client Statement 4
I hear your frustration. (Criterion 1) It's hard to feel this level of misery and to not be able to find relief. (Criterion 2)
Example Response to Advanced Client Statement 5
Sounds like you're worried I'm going to give up on you. (Criterion 1) It probably feels pretty hard to trust that I'm going to stick around, especially if you've h ad the experience of other therapists leaving you. (Criterion 2)

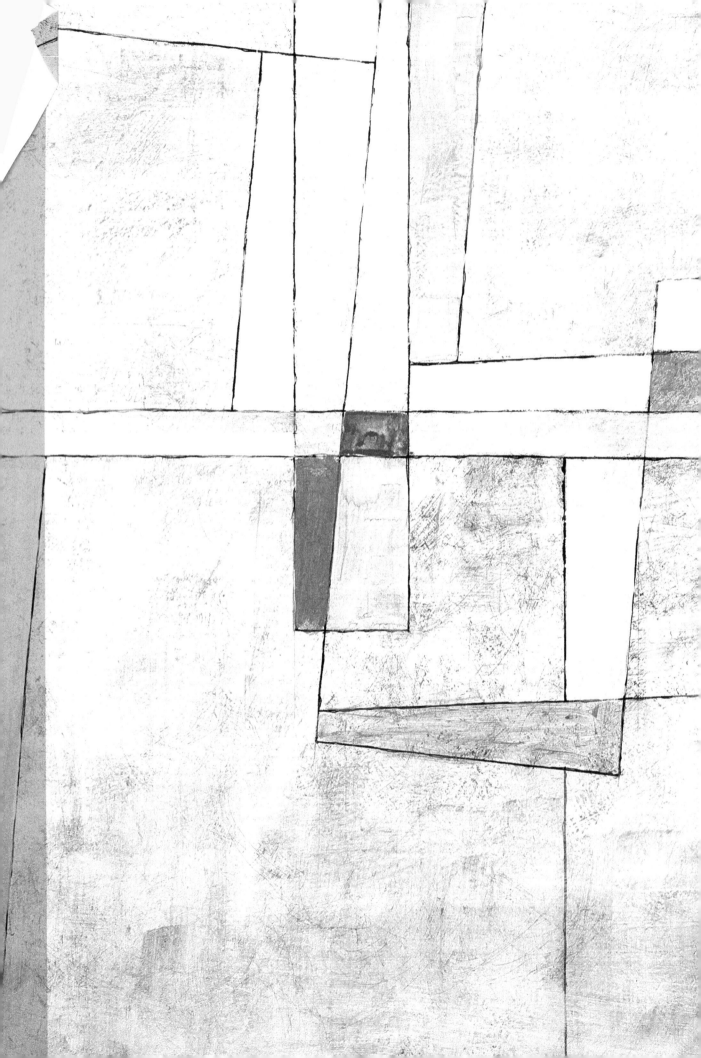

Reinforcing Adaptive Behaviors

Preparations for Exercise 3

1. Read the instructions in Chapter 2.

2. Download the Deliberate Practice Reaction Form and Deliberate Practice Diary Form at https://www.apa.org/pubs/books/deliberate-practice-dialectical-behavior-therapy (see the "Clinician and Practitioner Resources" tab; also available in Appendixes A and B, respectively).

Skill Description

Skill Difficulty Level: Beginner

Reinforcement of specific client behaviors is used in dialectical behavior therapy (DBT) to strengthen adaptive behaviors. An important learning principle associated with reinforcement is shaping. In shaping a behavioral response, gradual approximations toward the target behavior are reinforced; the DBT therapist reinforces any small step along the way toward a desired goal behavior. One of the most potent reinforcers is the therapeutic relationship. Linehan (1993a, 1993b) described the following relationship behaviors as potentially reinforcing: (a) expressions of the therapist's approval, care, concern, and interest; (b) therapist behaviors that communicate liking or admiring the client, or a desire to work or interact with the client; (c) behaviors that reassure the client that the therapist is dependable and the therapy secure; (d) validating responses; (e) behaviors that are responsive to a client's requests; and (f) attention from or contact with the therapist. Behaviors that arise in the therapist's presence allow for immediate reinforcement by the therapist; immediate consequences are more potent than delayed consequences. Accordingly, how a therapist responds to their client can influence subsequent client behavior and the likelihood that behavior will recur in the future.

https://doi.org/10.1037/0000322-005

Deliberate Practice in Dialectical Behavior Therapy, by T. Boritz, S. McMain, A. Vaz, and T. Rousmaniere

SKILL CRITERION FOR EXERCISE 3
1. The therapist conveys care, approval, appreciation, or validation in response to any adaptive or functional behavior.

Examples of Reinforcing Adaptive Behaviors

Example 1

CLIENT: [*Withdrawn*] I'm just feeling done with everything. Everything's a battle, and I'm exhausted. It took everything in me just to come in today.

THERAPIST: I am so glad you did come, especially given how exhausted you're feeling.

Example 2

CLIENT: [*Ashamed*] Sometimes I get so frustrated with myself that I hit myself to feel a bit better. I tried to do some of the skills we talked about last week, but they didn't seem to help much.

THERAPIST: It's great you tried to use skills—that's a step in the right direction. We can spend some time today figuring out what was helpful and what was not so helpful about those skills.

Example 3

CLIENT: [*Frustrated*] You're not listening to me. This is hard! I just want to leave this session.

THERAPIST: I really appreciate you telling me how you're feeling and that you are having the urge to leave the session.

INSTRUCTIONS FOR EXERCISE 3

Step 1: Role-Play and Feedback

- The client says the first beginner client statement. The therapist improvises a response based on the skill criteria.
- The trainer (or, if not available, the client) provides brief feedback based on the skill criteria.
- The client then repeats the same statement, and the therapist again improvises a response. The trainer (or client) again provides brief feedback.

Step 2: Repeat

- Repeat Step 1 for all the statements at the current difficulty level (beginner, intermediate, or advanced).

Step 3: Assess and Adjust Difficulty

- The therapist completes the Deliberate Practice Reaction Form (see Appendix A) and decides whether to make the exercise easier or harder or to repeat the same difficulty level.

Step 4: Repeat for Approximately 15 Minutes

- Repeat Steps 1 to 3 for at least 15 minutes.
- The trainees then switch therapist and client roles and start over.

> **Now it's your turn! Follow Steps 1 and 2 from the instructions.**

Remember: The goal of the role-play is for trainees to practice improvising responses to the client statements in a manner that (a) uses the skill criteria and (b) feels authentic for the trainee. **Example therapist responses for each client statement are provided at the end of this exercise. Trainees should attempt to improvise their own responses before reading the example responses.**

BEGINNER-LEVEL CLIENT STATEMENTS FOR EXERCISE 3
Beginner Client Statement 1
[Angry] The week was going well, and I felt like I was being so skillful, but then on Wednesday I asked my partner a simple question about getting together on the weekend, and she exploded at me.
Beginner Client Statement 2
[Sad] I feel like such a failure . . . I can't get a job, I can't find a partner. Everything is terrible and I'm such a loser. I try to not let it get to me, but I'm beginning to feel like I can't handle anything in this life.
Beginner Client Statement 3
[Discouraged] I've been working hard on keeping my drinking under control. I'm kind of nervous because my friend is having his birthday party at the bar this weekend and I really want to go but am worried I won't be able to resist drinking.
Beginner Client Statement 4
[Frustrated] I didn't want to come to session today. I had to really force myself.
Beginner Client Statement 5
[Happy] I had a good week. There were a few moments where I felt really bad and started to panic, but I was able to talk myself down. I was sort of surprised actually that the skills worked.

 Assess and adjust the difficulty before moving to the next difficulty level (see Step 3 in the exercise instructions).

INTERMEDIATE-LEVEL CLIENT STATEMENTS FOR EXERCISE 3
Intermediate Client Statement 1
[Angry] I want to quit the group. I feel like they're all judging me.
Intermediate Client Statement 2
[Sad] Last night I was feeling sad and just tried to let myself feel that feeling for a while. Usually, I'd try to distract myself. At some point, I kind of got bored and went downstairs to watch TV with my sister.
Intermediate Client Statement 3
[Angry] My mom just wouldn't stop nagging me. I tried to ask for space because I was getting really worked up, just like we talked about. But it didn't help. She just kept bothering me. Things sort of escalated from there and got pretty bad.
Intermediate Client Statement 4
[Hopeless] I just don't think I can do this homework on my own. Every time I sit down to do it, I get so overwhelmed.
Intermediate Client Statement 5
[Frustrated] When things get intense, I just act. I don't have any thoughts; I just react.

Assess and adjust the difficulty before moving to the next difficulty level (see Step 3 in the exercise instructions).

ADVANCED-LEVEL CLIENT STATEMENTS FOR EXERCISE 3
Advanced Client Statement 1
[Frustrated] You're not listening to me. This is hard! I just want to leave this session.
Advanced Client Statement 2
[Ashamed] I didn't complete my diary card. You're probably pissed I forgot again.
Advanced Client Statement 3
[Ashamed] I'm sorry for leaving you all those messages last week. I thought you were purposely ignoring my calls and just got really upset. When you called me back, I calmed down and felt really guilty about the messages.
Advanced Client Statement 4
[Angry] I'm so pissed today. The shit I've had to deal with this week is unbelievable. I'm just letting you know because I'm in a real mood today, so please don't test me.
Advanced Client Statement 5
[Ashamed] Sometimes I get so frustrated with myself that I hit myself to feel a bit better. I'm feeling so embarrassed even telling you about this.

Assess and adjust the difficulty here (see Step 3 in the exercise instructions). If appropriate, follow the instructions to make the exercise even more challenging (see Appendix A).

Example Therapist Responses: Reinforcing Adaptive Behaviors

Remember: Trainees should attempt to improvise their own responses before reading the example responses. **Do not read the following responses verbatim unless you are having trouble coming up with your own responses!**

EXAMPLE RESPONSES TO BEGINNER-LEVEL CLIENT STATEMENTS FOR EXERCISE 3
Example Response to Beginner Client Statement 1
I'm hearing that the week got hard, but before that you felt you were being skillful. I'd love to hear more about what you were doing that felt so effective.
Example Response to Beginner Client Statement 2
It's hard when those judgments and worry thoughts seep in. It's great that you're actively trying to interrupt them, hard as it may be to do.
Example Response to Beginner Client Statement 3
I'm so glad you're thinking ahead to the birthday party and some of the challenges that might come up in that environment. This gives us a chance to think through the situation together.
Example Response to Beginner Client Statement 4
It's especially great you made it in. It sounds like you had some pretty strong urges to avoid and acted opposite to them.
Example Response to Beginner Client Statement 5
This is fantastic news. It sounds like you were able to use skills in some really distressing moments and found it really helpful.

EXAMPLE RESPONSES TO INTERMEDIATE-LEVEL CLIENT STATEMENTS FOR EXERCISE 3

Example Response to Intermediate Client Statement 1

I'm really glad you're bringing up your urges to quit group rather than just doing it. It's hard to feel comfortable in a group if you feel like you're being judged, and maybe there's something we can figure out together that might help improve the situation.

Example Response to Intermediate Client Statement 2

Wow—it sounds like you tried to do something different this time. You let yourself feel sad, and when the feeling passed, you let it go. This sounds like a big step!

Example Response to Intermediate Client Statement 3

First things first—it's great that you tried to ask for space! It sounds like you noticed you were getting dysregulated and tried to deescalate the situation. That's really hard to do!

Example Response to Intermediate Client Statement 4

It sounds like you tried to do your homework multiple times this week, which is really wonderful. I'm glad you're talking about your difficulty doing the homework when you started feeling overwhelmed—this is absolutely something we can work on together.

Example Response to Intermediate Client Statement 5

Sounds like you were really on top of using skills when you started feeling your emotions getting intense. It also sounds like you were really mindful of how the breathing exercise you tried made you feel. It's great you were paying such close attention because now we can figure out how adjust or change that exercise so it's more effective for you.

EXAMPLE RESPONSES TO ADVANCED-LEVEL CLIENT STATEMENTS FOR EXERCISE 3
Example Response to Advanced Client Statement 1
I really appreciate you telling me how you're feeling right now. That's not easy to do, especially if you're feeling like I'm not hearing you properly. I also appreciate you telling me about your urge to leave rather than just acting on that urge.
Example Response to Advanced Client Statement 2
It sounds like you're worried about what I might be thinking about you right now. I'm glad you're bringing it up, rather than keeping those worry thoughts to yourself.
Example Response to Advanced Client Statement 3
Thank you for your apology. It sounds like in the moment, it was really hard to get unstuck from that upset feeling. It also sounds like you've had some time to reflect and are seeing things a bit differently now. Let's try to understand what happened together.
Example Response to Advanced Client Statement 4
I'm hearing it's been a hard week. I appreciate you telling me how you're feeling right now—it sounds like you're still feeling a bit vulnerable and are worried about getting set off in our session?
Example Response to Advanced Client Statement 5
I think it's really important that you told me, especially given that it felt embarrassing to do so.

Problem Assessment

Preparations for Exercise 4

1. Read the instructions in Chapter 2.

2. Download the Deliberate Practice Reaction Form and Deliberate Practice Diary Form at https://www.apa.org/pubs/books/deliberate-practice-dialectical-behavior-therapy (see the "Clinician and Practitioner Resources" tab; also available in Appendixes A and B, respectively).

Skill Description

Skill Difficulty Level: Beginner

Problem solving is the core dialectical behavior therapy (DBT) change strategy. Problem solving involves (a) understanding problems as they occur and (b) seeking to address them with alternative and more adaptive solutions. Problem assessment is the first step in this process. The goal of problem assessment is to ascertain the function of a specific problem behavior. Once insight into the problem behavior is achieved, the client and therapist proceed to the next problem-solving task, which includes generating and implementing problem solutions (e.g., skills training, exposure-based techniques, cognitive modification).

The *behavioral chain analysis* is the main tool used in problem assessment. A behavioral chain analysis is used to obtain a detailed understanding of the antecedents and consequences (i.e., the controlling variables) of a discrete episode of a specific behavior to determine what factors need to be problem solved. Controlling variables include contextual factors that link (a) antecedents and the problem behavior (i.e., vulnerability factors; prompting events; cognitions, emotions, actions, sensations) and (b) the problem behavior and its consequences (i.e., the internal and environmental responses that follow the problem behavior).

https://doi.org/10.1037/0000322-006

Deliberate Practice in Dialectical Behavior Therapy, by T. Boritz, S. McMain, A. Vaz, and T. Rousmaniere

When assessing a problem, therapists engage with their clients in a collaborative and nonjudgmental manner to understand the variables controlling the problem (e.g., the client's thoughts, feelings, actions, or context). DBT therapists ask relevant questions to define the problem that needs to be addressed rather than assuming what the problem is. DBT therapists help the client define the problem by using specific versus general language. For example, if a client says their problem is that they "get angry and lose their temper all the time," the therapist will try to elicit a precise description of the behavior (e.g., "What do you mean by 'lose your temper'? What actually happens when you get angry?").

For the purposes of this exercise, we will focus on helping DBT trainees reflect a specific problem behavior the client is reporting and ask relevant questions to help them clarify what contributed to the behavior.

SKILL CRITERIA FOR EXERCISE 4

1. The therapist reflects a specific problem that the client is reporting.
2. The therapist asks relevant questions to help the client clarify what contributed to the problem behavior (e.g., what happened prior to engaging in the problem behavior).

COMMON MISTAKES

1. The therapist responds in a global or vague manner.
2. The therapist makes assumptions about the client's problem.
3. The therapist engages in problem solving without clearly specifying the problem that needs to be addressed.
4. The therapist's tone and language demand an explanation of the problem (i.e., why the person responded the way they did) rather than cultivating curiosity in the client to understand and increase awareness.

Examples of Problem Assessment

Example 1

CLIENT: [*Neutral*] I didn't fill in my diary card. I thought about it, though.

THERAPIST: It sounds like you thought about your diary card this week, but something got in the way of actually completing it. (Criterion 1) What got in the way of filling out the diary card this week? (Criterion 2)

> **Common Therapist Mistake 1:** The therapist responds in a global or vague manner: What gets in the way of you doing your homework in this therapy?

Example 2

CLIENT: [*Ashamed*] I totally screwed up at work. I let my anger get out of control.

THERAPIST: It sounds like something happened at work that got you angry. (Criterion 1) When you say your anger got out of control, what exactly did you do? (Criterion 2)

Common Therapist Mistake 2: The therapist makes assumptions about the client problem: It sounds like your anger is a big problem and leading to all sorts of negative outcomes in your life.

Example 3

CLIENT: [*Angry*] When you say that, it's like you're telling me I'm lying.

THERAPIST: It sounds like something I said is making you think I don't believe you. (Criterion 1) What was it about what I said or how I came across to you right now that made you think that? (Criterion 2)

Common Therapist Mistake 3: The therapist engages in problem solving without assessing the problem that needs to be addressed: I'm not thinking that at all. I am wondering if we can work on challenging those negative thoughts when they pop up?

Example 4

CLIENT: [*Anxious*] I didn't go to group this week. I just didn't feel like it.

THERAPIST: You had group this week but didn't go. (Criterion 1) Can you tell me more about what you mean when you say you didn't feel like going? (Criterion 2)

Common Therapist Mistake 4: The therapist's tone and language demand an explanation of the problem: Why didn't you go?

INSTRUCTIONS FOR EXERCISE 4

Step 1: Role-Play and Feedback

- The client says the first beginner client statement. The therapist improvises a response based on the skill criteria.
- The trainer (or, if not available, the client) provides brief feedback based on the skill criteria.
- The client then repeats the same statement, and the therapist again improvises a response. The trainer (or client) again provides brief feedback.

Step 2: Repeat

- Repeat Step 1 for all the statements at the current difficulty level (beginner, intermediate, or advanced).

Step 3: Assess and Adjust Difficulty

- The therapist completes the Deliberate Practice Reaction Form (see Appendix A) and decides whether to make the exercise easier or harder or to repeat the same difficulty level.

Step 4: Repeat for Approximately 15 Minutes

- Repeat Steps 1 to 3 for at least 15 minutes.
- The trainees then switch therapist and client roles and start over.

Now it's your turn! Follow Steps 1 and 2 from the instructions.

Remember: The goal of the role-play is for trainees to practice improvising responses to the client statements in a manner that (a) uses the skill criteria and (b) feels authentic for the trainee. **Example therapist responses for each client statement are provided at the end of this exercise. Trainees should attempt to improvise their own responses before reading the example responses.**

BEGINNER-LEVEL CLIENT STATEMENTS FOR EXERCISE 4
Beginner Client Statement 1
[Angry] I want to quit group. I feel like they're all judging me.
Beginner Client Statement 2
[Sad] It was a really hard week, and if I'm being honest, I really considered cancelling our session today.
Beginner Client Statement 3
[Irritated] I didn't understand the homework. I tried to do it but gave up because none of it made any sense to me.
Beginner Client Statement 4
[Withdrawn] I don't really know what to say right now. I'm just feeling a bit numb.
Beginner Client Statement 5
[Ashamed] I got into a huge fight with my mom. She wouldn't leave me alone, and it just got so intense. I yelled at her and she backed off, but I came so close to hitting her.

Assess and adjust the difficulty before moving to the next difficulty level (see Step 3 in the exercise instructions).

INTERMEDIATE-LEVEL CLIENT STATEMENTS FOR EXERCISE 4
Intermediate Client Statement 1
[Frustrated] You don't get it—I'd use skills if I could, but when I get anxious, I go from zero to 100. There's no time to use skills!
Intermediate Client Statement 2
[Sad] I've been working really hard in this therapy. I feel like I've been making a lot of changes, but I still think about dying most days.
Intermediate Client Statement 3
[Ashamed] I'm sorry I missed last session. I really value your time, I just forgot. I really hope you're not mad at me.
Intermediate Client Statement 4
[Angry] I was really upset after our session. You ended our session so abruptly. I was so upset and you just sent me away.
Intermediate Client Statement 5
[Sad] I'm just feeling so overwhelmed. I can't even focus right now. I feel like I'm going to have a panic attack.

Assess and adjust the difficulty before moving to the next difficulty level (see Step 3 in the exercise instructions).

ADVANCED-LEVEL CLIENT STATEMENTS FOR EXERCISE 4
Advanced Client Statement 1
[Angry] I'm telling you I'm suicidal and you're telling me to grab an ice pack. How is that going to help me?
Advanced Client Statement 2
[Sad] I'm just not sure I can do this treatment. It's too hard. I've got kids. I can't fall apart right now.
Advanced Client Statement 3
[Ashamed] I tried using skills, but I felt suicidal all week. I tried to distract myself, but the thoughts kept coming. It's just too much. I can't live like this.
Advanced Client Statement 4
[Regret] I got mad at my friend for cancelling plans and sort of lost it on her. I screwed it all up.
Advanced Client Statement 5
[Irritated] I told you in my email I want to switch therapists. I don't really know why we had to have a session to talk about this.

Assess and adjust the difficulty here (see Step 3 in the exercise instructions). If appropriate, follow the instructions to make the exercise even more challenging (see Appendix A).

Example Therapist Responses: Problem Assessment

Remember: Trainees should attempt to improvise their own responses before reading the example responses. **Do not read the following responses verbatim unless you are having trouble coming up with your own responses!**

EXAMPLE RESPONSES TO BEGINNER-LEVEL CLIENT STATEMENTS FOR EXERCISE 4
Example Response to Beginner Client Statement 1
You are feeling judged and that's making you want to quit the group. (Criterion 1) Can we figure out what happened that left you thinking you're being judged and is now leading you to want to quit group? (Criterion 2)
Example Response to Beginner Client Statement 2
It sounds like it's been a tough week. (Criterion 1) What were you feeling that made you consider not coming? (Criterion 2)
Example Response to Beginner Client Statement 3
It sounds like you had a difficult time with the homework. (Criterion 1) I wonder if we can figure out together what it was about the homework that made you just want to avoid it? (Criterion 2)
Example Response to Beginner Client Statement 4
It sounds like it's hard to know what to say when everything inside is feeling kind of numb. (Criterion 1) I wonder if we can explore that feeling a bit more together? When did you notice that numb feeling was starting? (Criterion 2)
Example Response to Beginner Client Statement 5
It sounds like things got pretty heated between you and your mom. (Criterion 1) I wonder if we can spend some time talking about what happened that got your emotions so high in that interaction? (Criterion 2)

EXAMPLE RESPONSES TO INTERMEDIATE-LEVEL CLIENT STATEMENTS FOR EXERCISE 4
Example Response to Intermediate Client Statement 1
It sounds like when I start talking about skills it feels like I'm suggesting you're not trying. (Criterion 1) Can you tell me more about what you were thinking or feeling when I started bringing up skills? (Criterion 2)
Example Response to Intermediate Client Statement 2
It sounds like you're noticing your mind still wanders toward thoughts of suicide even though there's a lot of good stuff happening in your life right now. (Criterion 1) Can you tell me a bit more about the last time you noticed your mind go toward suicide? What was happening right before those thoughts of suicide popped up? (Criterion 2)
Example Response to Intermediate Client Statement 3
It sounds like you were planning on coming but then something happened that derailed the plan. (Criterion 1) I'd like to understand that better. What got in the way of making it into session last week? (Criterion 2)
Example Response to Intermediate Client Statement 4
It sounds like you felt very hurt by the way our last session ended. (Criterion 1) I wonder if you can tell me a bit about how you're feeling right now, as you're telling me this? (Criterion 2)
Example Response to Intermediate Client Statement 5
It sounds like you are experiencing a lot of emotion right now. (Criterion 1) Do you have a sense of what activated that feeling of overwhelm just now? What was happening inside just before you started feeling that way? (Criterion 2)

EXAMPLE RESPONSES TO ADVANCED-LEVEL CLIENT STATEMENTS FOR EXERCISE 4
Example Response to Advanced Client Statement 1
It sounds like it's feeling like you're in a house on fire and I'm offering you a glass of water to help with the heat. (Criterion 1) What thoughts or feelings came up when I asked you to grab an ice pack? (Criterion 2)
Example Response to Advanced Client Statement 2
It sounds like you're worried about being able to cope once we start opening stuff up in treatment. (Criterion 1) How did you get from having those worry thoughts to wanting to stop treatment? (Criterion 2)
Example Response to Advanced Client Statement 3
It sounds like despite using skills, the suicidal thoughts kept coming. (Criterion 1) What's so distressing or intolerable about those thoughts that makes you feel like you need to stop them or find some way to escape them? (Criterion 2)
Example Response to Advanced Client Statement 4
It sounds like you wish things had gone differently. (Criterion 1) Do you have a sense of what got activated in you when she cancelled plans, and how that then led to you "losing it" on her? (Criterion 2)
Example Response to Advanced Client Statement 5
It sounds like you don't see a reason for this session. (Criterion 1) I want to understand better what's going on that's leading you to want to change therapists. Can you tell me a bit about how you've been feeling in our sessions and what led you to ask for a new therapist? (Criterion 2)

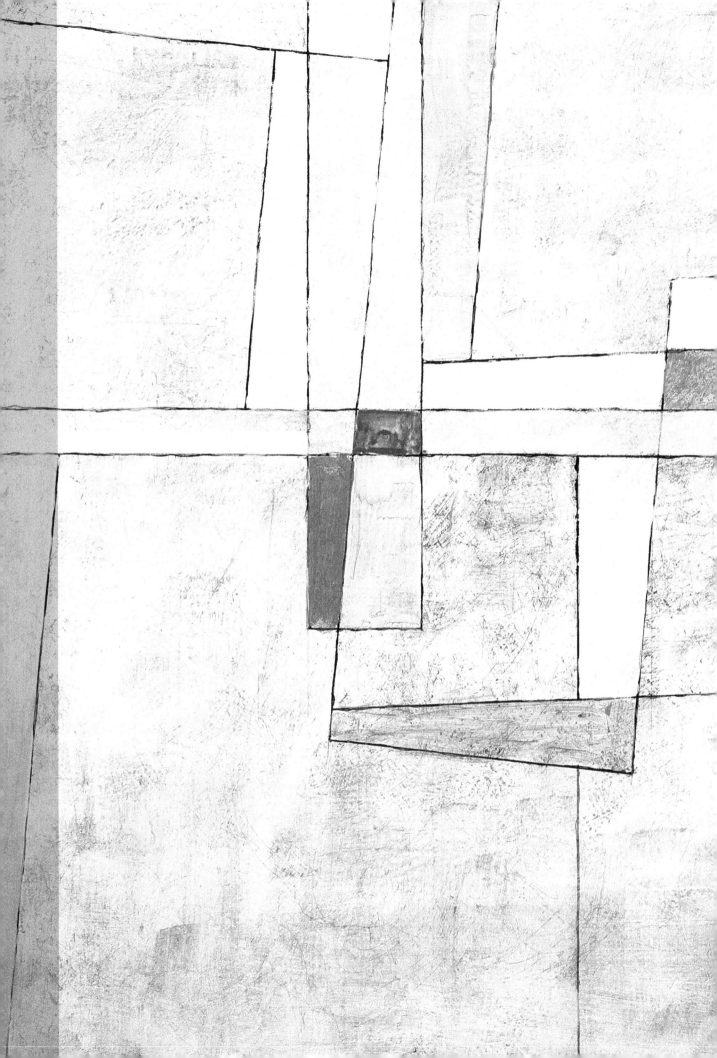

Eliciting a Commitment

Preparations for Exercise 5

1. Read the instructions in Chapter 2.

2. Download the Deliberate Practice Reaction Form and Deliberate Practice Diary Form at https://www.apa.org/pubs/books/deliberate-practice-dialectical-behavior-therapy (see the "Clinician and Practitioner Resources" tab; also available in Appendixes A and B, respectively).

Skill Description

Skill Difficulty Level: Intermediate

In dialectical behavior therapy (DBT), therapists actively seek explicit and collaborative agreement from the client to work toward mutually determined goals. An important task of DBT therapists is to help clients increase their motivation to make changes, particularly in moments when ambivalence or reluctance to change is high. Motivation and commitment naturally fluctuate over time, and when this occurs, the therapist's role is to help the client reconnect to their original commitment and a renewed effort to change.

Commitment strategies are used to help clients make an explicit intention to change, which increases the likelihood of taking action on a plan. When working to enhance motivation and commitment, therapists must be careful not to impose their own goals on the client or to demand their clients commit to a goal they had previously endorsed. Although there are a wide range of commitment strategies therapists can use in DBT, for the purposes of this exercise, we focus mainly on the practice of eliciting a commitment via checking in with the client about their willingness to work on a specific goal, use a particular skill, or their engage in a particular therapeutic task.

https://doi.org/10.1037/0000322-007

SKILL CRITERIA FOR EXERCISE 5
1. The therapist highlights a specific opportunity for behavioral change.
2. Based on the client's statement, the therapist invites/asks the client to commit to working on changing a specific behavior.

Examples of Eliciting a Commitment

Example 1

CLIENT: [*Guilty*] I've been feeling really bad about how I've been treating my partner. Lately I'm just finding everything he says very annoying, and I can't stop myself from starting fights with him that just escalate.

THERAPIST: It sounds like in moments where you're feeling really annoyed, you're finding that you can't control your anger. (Criterion 1) I'm wondering if you're interested in understanding your reaction and trying to figure out ways not to lose your cool even if you are irritated with your partner? (Criterion 2)

Example 2

CLIENT: [*Ashamed*] Sometimes I get so frustrated with myself that I hit myself to feel a bit better.

THERAPIST: It sounds like you're overwhelmed with self-criticism and frustration and hitting yourself is the only way you can think of to relieve the intensity of this state. (Criterion 1) Are you willing to work with me to find more helpful ways to deal with your self-criticism that don't involve hitting yourself? (Criterion 2)

Example 3

CLIENT: [*Worried*] I'm so worried that I won't be able to pay my bills next month, and I don't even know what I can do about it. It's overwhelming, and honestly I just want to give up and kill myself.

THERAPIST: It sounds like there's a lot going on right now that's leaving you feeling helpless and your mind is escaping into thoughts of suicide. (Criterion 1) Are you willing to work together to find ways to not act on suicide thoughts and to help you feel more in control? (Criterion 2)

INSTRUCTIONS FOR EXERCISE 5

Step 1: Role-Play and Feedback

- The client says the first beginner client statement. The therapist improvises a response based on the skill criteria.
- The trainer (or, if not available, the client) provides brief feedback based on the skill criteria.
- The client then repeats the same statement, and the therapist again improvises a response. The trainer (or client) again provides brief feedback.

Step 2: Repeat

- Repeat Step 1 for all the statements at the current difficulty level (beginner, intermediate, or advanced).

Step 3: Assess and Adjust Difficulty

- The therapist completes the Deliberate Practice Reaction Form (see Appendix A) and decides whether to make the exercise easier or harder or to repeat the same difficulty level.

Step 4: Repeat for Approximately 15 Minutes

- Repeat Steps 1 to 3 for at least 15 minutes.
- The trainees then switch therapist and client roles and start over.

> **Now it's your turn! Follow Steps 1 and 2 from the instructions.**

Remember: The goal of the role-play is for trainees to practice improvising responses to the client statements in a manner that (a) uses the skill criteria and (b) feels authentic for the trainee. **Example therapist responses for each client statement are provided at the end of this exercise. Trainees should attempt to improvise their own responses before reading the example responses.**

BEGINNER-LEVEL CLIENT STATEMENTS FOR EXERCISE 5
Beginner Client Statement 1
[Angry] The week was going well, but then on Wednesday, I asked my partner a simple question about getting together on the weekend, and she exploded at me. At this point, I don't even know why I'm bothering to try so hard. Part of me just wants to call it quits on the relationship.
Beginner Client Statement 2
[Sad] I feel like such a failure . . . I can't get a job, I can't find a partner. Everything is terrible and I'm such a loser. I try to not let it get to me, but I'm beginning to feel like I can't handle anything in this life.
Beginner Client Statement 3
[Discouraged] I've been working hard on keeping my drinking under control. I'm kind of nervous because my friend is having his birthday party at the bar this weekend and I really want to go but am worried I won't be able to resist drinking.
Beginner Client Statement 4
[Frustrated] Sometimes I get so angry at myself that I hit myself.
Beginner Client Statement 5
[Neutral] My parents said that I need to be more independent of them. They said I should come see you to work on that.

 Assess and adjust the difficulty before moving to the next difficulty level (see Step 3 in the exercise instructions).

INTERMEDIATE-LEVEL CLIENT STATEMENTS FOR EXERCISE 5
Intermediate Client Statement 1
[Angry] My doctor said I have to come see you about my "anger problem." Sometimes when I get really angry, I lose control and hit people. I just get so angry when people say stupid things!
Intermediate Client Statement 2
[Irritated] You're the expert, why don't you just tell me what you think I should do.
Intermediate Client Statement 3
[Anxious] I can't commit to coming in here each week. My schedule is unpredictable, and I don't have a car.
Intermediate Client Statement 4
[Hopeless] I just don't think I can do this homework on my own.
Intermediate Client Statement 5
[Frustrated] I don't know . . . when things get intense, I just act. I don't have any thoughts; I just act or react.

Assess and adjust the difficulty before moving to the next difficulty level (see Step 3 in the exercise instructions).

ADVANCED-LEVEL CLIENT STATEMENTS FOR EXERCISE 5
Advanced Client Statement 1
[Angry] I think our sessions have been helpful, but my depression is getting worse. On my drive to session today, I pictured myself driving off a bridge. It honestly felt like a relief to imagine not having to work so hard to feel better anymore.
Advanced Client Statement 2
[Frustrated] You don't understand. I can't do these things because I'm anxious all the time. If I wasn't anxious, I could easily do these things and I wouldn't need to be here in the first place.
Advanced Client Statement 3
[Ashamed] I'm sorry for leaving you all those messages last week. I thought you were purposely ignoring my calls and just got really upset. When you called me back, I calmed down and felt really guilty about the messages.
Advanced Client Statement 4
[Sad] I just feel like giving up. Everything feels too hard and I'm just really tired of trying.
Advanced Client Statement 5
[Anxious] I think I need to drop my classes. I'm behind on all my deadlines and overwhelmed. And all my professors hate me.

> ✋ **Assess and adjust the difficulty here (see Step 3 in the exercise instructions). If appropriate, follow the instructions to make the exercise even more challenging (see Appendix A).**

Example Therapist Responses: Eliciting a Commitment

Remember: Trainees should attempt to improvise their own responses before reading the example responses. **Do not read the following responses verbatim unless you are having trouble coming up with your own responses!**

EXAMPLE RESPONSES TO BEGINNER-LEVEL CLIENT STATEMENTS FOR EXERCISE 5
Example Response to Beginner Client Statement 1
It sounds like something in that interaction went awry, and now you're left feeling pretty discouraged and want to give up. (Criterion 1) Are you willing to spend some time today looking back at what happened on Wednesday to see if we can understand it better? (Criterion 2)
Example Response to Beginner Client Statement 2
It sounds like you've got a list going of all the things that aren't working out and are getting pretty down on yourself. (Criterion 1) Are you willing to spend some time today to see if we can work on bringing down those judgments? (Criterion 2)
Example Response to Beginner Client Statement 3
It sounds like you've been working hard not to drink and here's a situation where there will be a lot of triggers for drinking. (Criterion 1) Given your goal is not to drink, how committed are you to doing everything in your power to not act on urges to drink? Can we spend some time today coming up with a solid plan for increasing the likelihood of not drinking? (Criterion 2)
Example Response to Beginner Client Statement 4
It sounds like when your anger gets pretty high, it can come with urges to hit yourself, which perhaps makes the anger settle down a bit in the moment. (Criterion 1) Is working on finding an alternative way of managing your anger and anger behaviors something you are willing to do in this therapy? (Criterion 2)
Example Response to Beginner Client Statement 5
It sounds like part of the reason you're here is because your parents said you should come to work on being more independent. (Criterion 1) Is being more independent something that you want to work on? (Criterion 2)

**EXAMPLE RESPONSES TO INTERMEDIATE-LEVEL
CLIENT STATEMENTS FOR EXERCISE 5**

Example Response to Intermediate Client Statement 1

Your doctor told you to get help for your anger, and it sounds like you're also aware that your anger can get intense and out of control at times. (Criterion 1) Are you willing to learn ways to not lose control of your anger? (Criterion 2)

Example Response to Intermediate Client Statement 2

You sound frustrated and like you really want some support right now. (Criterion 1) While I don't have a magical solution to offer, I'm willing to work with you to find a solution if that's something you're open to doing. (Criterion 2)

Example Response to Intermediate Client Statement 3

It sounds like you've got a lot going on and it seems impossible to imagine attending therapy on a regular basis. (Criterion 1) Are you willing to work with me to find a way to get here regularly so you can get the most out of therapy? (Criterion 2)

Example Response to Intermediate Client Statement 4

It sounds like you view yourself as someone who is not capable of doing this work on your own. (Criterion 1) I'm wondering if you'd be willing to act like that view of yourself—"I'm not capable"—is a belief and not a fact? (Criterion 2)

Example Response to Intermediate Client Statement 5

It's so hard to interrupt those urges to act when your emotions become intense. (Criterion 1) I'm wondering if you would be willing to work on trying to lower the intensity of your emotions before they start feeling out of control? (Criterion 2)

EXAMPLE RESPONSES TO ADVANCED-LEVEL CLIENT STATEMENTS FOR EXERCISE 5
Example Response to Advanced Client Statement 1
You sound emotionally exhausted and depressed, and I imagine it's hard to keep yourself motivated when you're in this state. (Criterion 1) Are you willing to work with me to find some ways to get some relief that don't involve suicide? (Criterion 2)
Example Response to Advanced Client Statement 2
I can hear how frustrated you feel that anxiety is getting in the way of doing the things you want to do. (Criterion 1) Are you willing to work with me to keep doing the things that will bring you some relief in the long run, even if it means tolerating that anxiety in the short run? (Criterion 2)
Example Response to Advanced Client Statement 3
It sounds like when I didn't respond, you got overwhelmed with intense feelings and it was hard to not call me repeatedly. (Criterion 1) Would you be willing to explore what emotions got activated when I didn't respond, and how you might be able to regulate those feelings in the future? (Criterion 2)
Example Response to Advanced Client Statement 4
It sounds like things are feeling really hard right now and there's a part of you that's so tired you just want to stop trying. (Criterion 1) Are you willing to work with me to find ways of lightening your load without giving up? (Criteria 2)
Example Response to Advanced Client Statement 5
It sounds like you're upset with yourself for being behind at school and are really judging yourself. (Criterion 1) I'm wondering if you would be willing to notice how you're talking to yourself and drop those judgments? (Criterion 2)

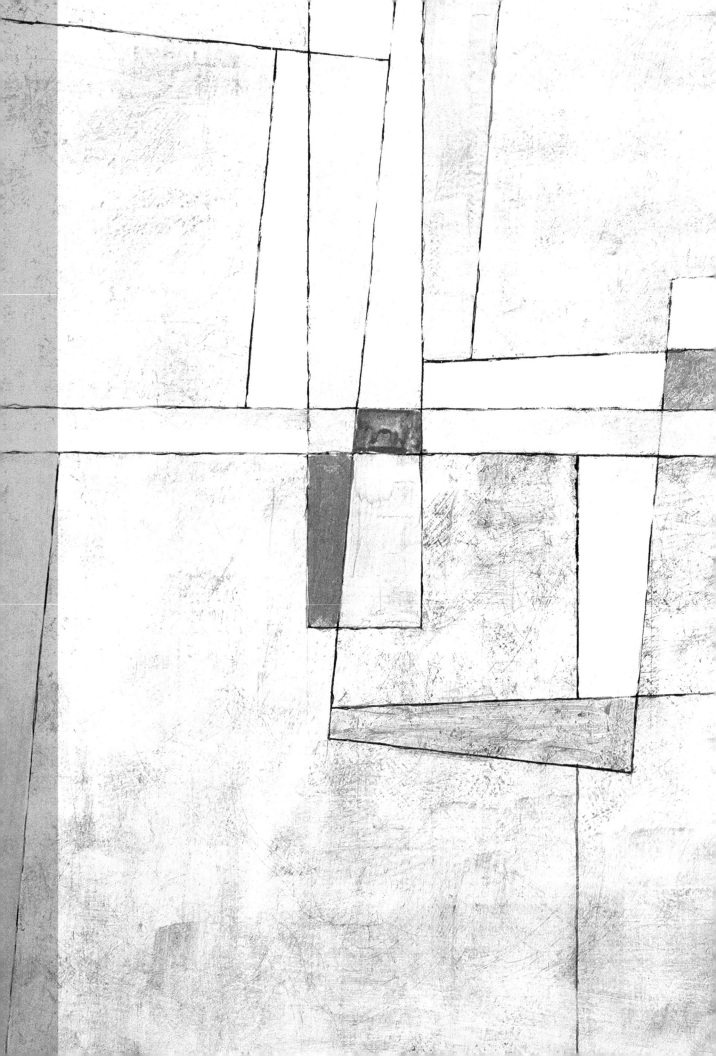

Inviting the Client to Engage in Problem Solving

Preparations for Exercise 6

1. Read the instructions in Chapter 2.

2. Download the Deliberate Practice Reaction Form and Deliberate Practice Diary Form at https://www.apa.org/pubs/books/deliberate-practice-dialectical-behavior-therapy (see the "Clinician and Practitioner Resources" tab; also available in Appendixes A and B, respectively).

Skill Description

Skill Difficulty Level: Intermediate

In Exercise 4, we focused on problem assessment, which involved reflecting a specific problem behavior and asking relevant questions to clarify which variables are controlling the behavior. The next task in dialectical behavior therapy (DBT) is to proceed to generate and implement solutions to the problem (e.g., via skills training, exposure-based techniques, and cognitive modification). Problem solving involves helping the client brainstorm as many solutions to the problem as possible, including specific adaptive coping strategies to replace maladaptive coping strategies. It can be helpful for the therapist and client to evaluate the effectiveness of solutions to identify the short- and long-term consequences of various options. DBT therapists then help the client choose and implement a specific solution, identify any barriers that might occur to using the selected solution, and troubleshoot if their attempt to solve their problem goes wrong or new problems emerge.

Although there are a wide range of problem-solving strategies that DBT therapists can use, for the purposes of this exercise, we will focus mainly on the practice of highlighting a maladaptive coping strategy or problematic behavior and inviting the client to use an adaptive coping response to replace a problematic behavior.

https://doi.org/10.1037/0000322-008

SKILL CRITERIA FOR EXERCISE 6
1. The therapist highlights a maladaptive coping strategy or problematic behavior in a nonjudgmental manner.
2. The therapist invites the client to engage in an adaptive coping response to replace a problematic behavior.

Examples of Inviting the Client to Engage in Problem Solving

Example 1

CLIENT: [*Neutral*] I didn't fill in my diary card. Every time I looked at it, I felt overwhelmed.

THERAPIST: It sounds like when you started doing the diary card, some intense emotions got activated, and it brought some relief to stop doing the diary card. (Criterion 1) Would you like some help figuring out how to manage those overwhelming feelings rather than avoiding them? (Criterion 2)

Example 2

CLIENT: [*Ashamed*] I totally screwed up at work. I let my anger get out of control and yelled at my boss.

THERAPIST: That's too bad. It sounds like something happened that set off your anger and once it was activated, it was hard to control those anger behaviors. (Criterion 1) Perhaps we can spend some time today figuring out some skills to help interrupt anger urges when your emotion is really high. What do you think about that? (Criterion 2)

Example 3

CLIENT: [*Angry*] When you say that, it's like you're telling me I'm lying. I just want to leave right now.

THERAPIST: I can see you're feeling frustrated with me right now. I'm thinking that leaving the session might be one way of managing that feeling. (Criterion 1) I wonder if you want some help bringing the intensity of that feeling down a bit, so we can talk more about what I said or did that made you feel like I didn't believe you. (Criterion 2)

INSTRUCTIONS FOR EXERCISE 6
Step 1: Role-Play and Feedback
• The client says the first beginner client statement. The therapist improvises a response based on the skill criteria.
• The trainer (or, if not available, the client) provides brief feedback based on the skill criteria.
• The client then repeats the same statement, and the therapist again improvises a response. The trainer (or client) again provides brief feedback.
Step 2: Repeat
• Repeat Step 1 for all the statements at the current difficulty level (beginner, intermediate, or advanced).
Step 3: Assess and Adjust Difficulty
• The therapist completes the Deliberate Practice Reaction Form (see Appendix A) and decides whether to make the exercise easier or harder or to repeat the same difficulty level.
Step 4: Repeat for Approximately 15 Minutes
• Repeat Steps 1 to 3 for at least 15 minutes.
• The trainees then switch therapist and client roles and start over.

> **Now it's your turn! Follow Steps 1 and 2 from the instructions.**

Remember: The goal of the role-play is for trainees to practice improvising responses to the client statements in a manner that (a) uses the skill criteria and (b) feels authentic for the trainee. **Example therapist responses for each client statement are provided at the end of this exercise. Trainees should attempt to improvise their own responses before reading the example responses.**

BEGINNER-LEVEL CLIENT STATEMENTS FOR EXERCISE 6
Beginner Client Statement 1
[Angry] I want to quit group. I feel like they're all judging me.
Beginner Client Statement 2
[Sad] It was a really hard week, and if I'm being honest, I really considered cancelling our session today. I don't think you're going to be able to help me.
Beginner Client Statement 3
[Irritated] I didn't understand the homework. I tried to do it but gave up because none of it made any sense to me.
Beginner Client Statement 4
[Withdrawn] I don't really know what to say right now. I'm just feeling a bit numbed out and fuzzy.
Beginner Client Statement 5
[Ashamed] I got into a huge fight with my mom last night. She wouldn't leave me alone, and it just got so intense. I yelled at her and she backed off, but I came so close to hitting her.

 Assess and adjust the difficulty before moving to the next difficulty level (see Step 3 in the exercise instructions).

INTERMEDIATE-LEVEL CLIENT STATEMENTS FOR EXERCISE 6
Intermediate Client Statement 1
[Frustrated] I feel like I get bullied a lot by my family. Like I'm the butt of every joke. They only stop when I lose my temper. But now they're like, "You have an anger problem." They don't get it.
Intermediate Client Statement 2
[Sad] I've been working really hard in this therapy. I feel like I've been making a lot of good changes, but I still think about dying most days. And once I start thinking about suicide, it just opens the gate and I can't stop the thoughts.
Intermediate Client Statement 3
[Anxious] I'm just not sure I can do this treatment. It's too hard. I've got kids. I can't fall apart right now.
Intermediate Client Statement 4
[Sad] I got mad at my friend for cancelling plans and sort of lost it on her. I'm pretty sure I ruined that relationship. Nothing new. I suck at keeping friends.
Intermediate Client Statement 5
[Ashamed] I just felt empty. Nothing else was helping so I cut myself and the pain felt good. Like I could feel something.

 Assess and adjust the difficulty before moving to the next difficulty level (see Step 3 in the exercise instructions).

ADVANCED-LEVEL CLIENT STATEMENTS FOR EXERCISE 6
Advanced Client Statement 1
[Anxious] You said you were going to be there for me and now you're telling me you're going on vacation for 2 weeks? Maybe I should just quit now.
Advanced Client Statement 2
[Angry] I'm so pissed today. The shit I've had to deal with this week is unbelievable. I'm just letting you know because I'm in a real mood today so please don't test me.
Advanced Client Statement 3
[Sad] I tried so hard to make things better with my boyfriend, but it wasn't enough. He broke up with me anyway. I'm just ready to give up.
Advanced Client Statement 4
[Angry] This is bullshit! I told you what the problem is, and you just don't want to help me. Breathing is not going to help me with my eviction notice. That is what I need help with.
Advanced Client Statement 5
[Ashamed] I tried using skills, but this week was just too hard. It's just too much. I can't live like this. I don't want to be here anymore.

> ✋ **Assess and adjust the difficulty here (see Step 3 in the exercise instructions). If appropriate, follow the instructions to make the exercise even more challenging (see Appendix A).**

Example Therapist Responses: Inviting the Client to Engage in Problem Solving

Remember: Trainees should attempt to improvise their own responses before reading the example responses. **Do not read the following responses verbatim unless you are having trouble coming up with your own responses!**

EXAMPLE RESPONSES TO BEGINNER-LEVEL CLIENT STATEMENTS FOR EXERCISE 6
Example Response to Beginner Client Statement 1
If I thought I was being judged, I might want to avoid something too. (Criterion 1) Quitting group is one way to solve the problem, but we could also try to figure out together some skills you can use in group so it doesn't feel so aversive. What do you think about that? (Criterion 2)
Example Response to Beginner Client Statement 2
It sounds like there's a part of you that's feeling a bit hopeless that I'll be able to help. (Criterion 1) Since you showed up today, I'm guessing there's the other part, though, that's acting opposite to the urge to give up. How can we keep that "not giving up" part mobilized so we can talk more about what made this week so hard and see if we can problem solve some of those challenges together? (Criterion 2)
Example Response to Beginner Client Statement 3
It sounds like you were trying to do the homework and at some point, it just started to feel super frustrating. (Criterion 1) I wonder if we can make a plan for homework this week that includes what to do if it's confusing or your frustration is getting too high and you have urges to just stop doing it? (Criterion 2)
Example Response to Beginner Client Statement 4
It sounds like the numbed-out, dissociative feeling is making it a bit hard to engage with me right now. (Criterion 1) Do you want some help using skills to get more present with me? (Criterion 2)
Example Response to Beginner Client Statement 5
It sounds like you're feeling pretty badly about what happened last night. (Criterion 1) It also sounds like it might be helpful for us to spend some time today focusing on how to manage those anger urges and communicate more effectively with your mom. Does that seem like something that could be a helpful focus for today? (Criterion 2)

EXAMPLE RESPONSES TO INTERMEDIATE-LEVEL CLIENT STATEMENTS FOR EXERCISE 6

Example Response to Intermediate Client Statement 1

It makes sense that you kind of maintain that angry state around them, if you feel that's the only way you're able to get some relief from the bullying and feel safe. (Criterion 1) What do you think about spending time today coming up with a plan for how to communicate this pattern to your family to see if it's something that can be worked on? Is that something you would want to do? (Criterion 2)

Example Response to Intermediate Client Statement 2

It sounds like you're noticing your mind still wanders toward thoughts of suicide—almost like a habitual response—but then it gets hard to stop more thoughts, and that feels pretty discouraging. (Criterion 1) Do you want to some help figuring out how to interrupt the suicide thoughts when they come up instead of sinking further into them? (Criterion 2)

Example Response to Intermediate Client Statement 3

This sounds really important. You're worried that doing this treatment is going to make it hard to be there for your kids. (Criterion 1) Do you think it would help if we came up with a plan for helping you cope if things get tough for you in treatment? (Criterion 2)

Example Response to Intermediate Client Statement 4

Something about your friend cancelling plans really upset you. (Criterion 1) I wonder if we can spend some time today figuring out what was so upsetting and a more effective way of handling that feeling when it gets activated? (Criterion 2)

Example Response to Intermediate Client Statement 5

It sounds like for you that empty feeling is really unbearable, and cutting helped get rid of it. (Criterion 1) Do you want to spend some time today figuring out a different way of dealing with that empty feeling? (Criterion 2)

EXAMPLE RESPONSES TO ADVANCED-LEVEL CLIENT STATEMENTS FOR EXERCISE 6
Example Response to Advanced Client Statement 1
It makes sense you're feeling a bit worried about me going away. (Criterion 1) Do you think it would help if we came up with a plan in advance for skills you can use or other supports we can put in place while I'm away? (Criterion 2)
Example Response to Advanced Client Statement 2
It sounds like you're feeling pretty vulnerable after a tough week and don't want to feel any worse today. (Criterion 1) Is there anything I can do right now to help you feel less overwhelmed? (Criterion 2)
Example Response to Advanced Client Statement 3
It sounds like you're feeling really sad about your breakup and are feeling kind of hopeless. (Criterion 1) I wonder if we can look at ways to help you grieve your relationship without moving into that giving-up state? (Criterion 2)
Example Response to Advanced Client Statement 4
It's really hard to be in so much distress and to feel like no one's listening or trying to help. (Criterion 1) Would it be helpful if we spent some time figuring out the eviction notice together and planning what you're going to do next? (Criterion 2)
Example Response to Advanced Client Statement 5
It sounds like you're in a lot of pain, and thinking about not being here anymore feels like the only escape. (Criterion 1) If we can come up with some other ways to help you with that suffering, would you be open to doing some problem solving with me? (Criterion 2)

Skills Training

Preparations for Exercise 7

1. Read the instructions in Chapter 2.

2. Download the Deliberate Practice Reaction Form and Deliberate Practice Diary Form at https://www.apa.org/pubs/books/deliberate-practice-dialectical-behavior-therapy (see the "Clinician and Practitioner Resources" tab; also available in Appendixes A and B, respectively).

Skill Description

Skill Difficulty Level: Intermediate

Skills training is used in problem solving when a solution requires skills not currently in a client's behavioral repertoire (e.g., when the client does not yet have the ability to generate or effectively produce a specific behavior). An essential aim of dialectical behavior therapy (DBT) is to help clients replace ineffective or maladaptive behaviors with skillful or effective responses. The use of the term *effective* in this context refers to the consequences of the behavior—for example, behaviors that lead to "a maximum of positive outcomes with a minimum of negative outcomes" (Linehan, 1993a, p. 329). During skills training in DBT, the therapist highlights opportunities for the client to actively engage in the acquisition and practice of skills.

Although a range of coping skills are used in DBT skills training, for the purposes of this exercise, we focus on two specific DBT skills: (a) the core mindfulness "what" skills for enhancing awareness of thoughts, feelings, and behaviors (including action urges); and (b) the distress tolerance STOP skills for noticing when an emotion is high and accompanied by urges to act impulsively on ineffective behaviors.

https://doi.org/10.1037/0000322-009

Mindfulness Skills

In DBT, *mindfulness* is defined as paying attention in a particular way in the present moment without judgment. The mindfulness "what" skills explain what we do when we're trying to be mindful: we observe (i.e., notice what we are experiencing without judgment, reaction, or trying to change anything), describe (i.e., putting words to our experience), and participate (i.e., actively and fully focusing on whatever we are doing in the present moment). For each of these skills, we practice one at a time, focusing on bringing full attention to what we're doing in the present moment (i.e., acting "one-mindfully") and either observing, describing, or participating.

Distress Tolerance: The STOP Skill

The STOP skill is used when a person is in crisis or a moment of intense distress. This skill is used to help clients get through a crisis without engaging in problematic behaviors that will make the situation worse. The STOP skill is a mnemonic device that stands for: Stop (i.e., freeze in your tracks, don't move, don't react), Take a step back (i.e., take some time to calm down and think), Observe (i.e., notice what is happening around you and within you), and Proceed mindfully (i.e., ask yourself what you want from the situation, remind yourself of your goals, and evaluate which responses will make the situation better or worse).

SKILL CRITERIA FOR EXERCISE 7

1. The therapist highlights a maladaptive behavior in a nonjudgmental manner.
2. The therapist explains the problems with the maladaptive behavior or the benefits of adaptive coping behaviors.
3. The therapist invites the client to use one of the following coping skills to replace a problematic/ineffective behavior:

   Option 1: Invite the client to use mindfulness skills to gain awareness of thoughts, feelings, behaviors, and urges in a nonjudgmental manner.

   Option 2: Invite the client to use the STOP skill for noticing when emotion is high and they are having urges to act impulsively on unhelpful behaviors.

Examples of Skills Training

Example 1

CLIENT: [*Neutral*] I didn't fill in my diary card. Every time I looked at it, I felt overwhelmed. So I just stopped.

THERAPIST: It sounds like when you started doing the diary card some intense emotions got activated, and it brought you some relief to just stop doing the diary card. (Criterion 1) While avoiding your diary card will bring relief to uncomfortable emotions in the short term, learning to stay with and tolerate your emotions without escaping them will be more effective in the long term. (Criterion 2)

Option 1: Next time you're doing your diary card, it may be helpful to use the mindfulness skills to observe the emotions and urges that come up. What do you think about that? (Criterion 3)

Option 2: The STOP skills might be a perfect skill to use in moments when your emotions are high and you're feeling tempted to do something that may not be helpful. (Criterion 3)

Example 2

CLIENT: [*Ashamed*] I totally screwed up at work. I let my anger get out of control and yelled at my boss.

THERAPIST: That's too bad. It sounds like something happened that set off your anger and once it was activated it was hard to control those anger behaviors. (Criterion 1) It might be helpful in this case to work on feeling your emotions without acting on the urges associated with them, so as not to make the situation worse in the moment. (Criterion 2)

Option 1: Would you like some help using mindfulness skills to notice the intensity of your anger and the urges to act from this emotion? (Criterion 3)

Option 2: Would you like some help using the STOP skills when your anger is high so that you don't act impulsively and engage in anger behaviors? (Criterion 3)

Example 3

CLIENT: [*Angry*] It feels like you're telling me I'm lying. I just feel like leaving right now.

THERAPIST: I can see you're feeling frustrated with me right now. I'm thinking that leaving the session might be one way of managing that feeling. (Criterion 1) If we can help you bring the intensity of that feeling down a bit, we might be able to talk more about what I said or did just now that made you feel like I wasn't believing you. (Criterion 2)

Option 1: Can you use mindfulness skills to notice the emotions and urges coming up for you right now? (Criterion 3)

Option 2: Would you be willing to use the STOP skill right now to interrupt that urge to leave? (Criterion 3)

INSTRUCTIONS FOR EXERCISE 7

Step 1: Role-Play and Feedback

- The client says the first beginner client statement. The therapist improvises a response based on the skill criteria.
- The trainer (or, if not available, the client) provides brief feedback based on the skill criteria.
- The client then repeats the same statement, and the therapist again improvises a response. The trainer (or client) again provides brief feedback.

Step 2: Repeat

- Repeat Step 1 for all the statements at the current difficulty level (beginner, intermediate, or advanced).

Step 3: Assess and Adjust Difficulty

- The therapist completes the Deliberate Practice Reaction Form (see Appendix A) and decides whether to make the exercise easier or harder or to repeat the same difficulty level.

Step 4: Repeat for Approximately 15 Minutes

- Repeat Steps 1 to 3 for at least 15 minutes.
- The trainees then switch therapist and client roles and start over.

> **Now it's your turn! Follow Steps 1 and 2 from the instructions.**

Remember: The goal of the role-play is for trainees to practice improvising responses to the client statements in a manner that (a) uses the skill criteria and (b) feels authentic for the trainee. **Example therapist responses for each client statement are provided at the end of this exercise. Trainees should attempt to improvise their own responses before reading the example responses.**

BEGINNER-LEVEL CLIENT STATEMENTS FOR EXERCISE 7
Beginner Client Statement 1
[Sad] I feel like such a failure . . . I can't get a job; I can't find a partner. Everything is terrible and I'm such a loser. I try to not let it get to me, but I'm beginning to feel like I can't handle anything in this life.
Beginner Client Statement 2
[Discouraged] I've been working hard on keeping my drinking under control. I'm kind of nervous because my friend is having his birthday party at the bar this weekend and I really want to go but am worried I won't be able to resist drinking.
Beginner Client Statement 3
[Angry] I want to quit group. I feel like they're all judging me.
Beginner Client Statement 4
[Angry] My mom just wouldn't stop nagging me. I asked her to leave me alone, but she just kept going. So I got really in her face and screamed at her. I think I scared her. But I guess it worked because she backed off.
Beginner Client Statement 5
[Angry] My boss is such a jerk and I just want to quit this job.

 Assess and adjust the difficulty before moving to the next difficulty level (see Step 3 in the exercise instructions).

INTERMEDIATE-LEVEL CLIENT STATEMENTS FOR EXERCISE 7
Intermediate Client Statement 1
[Ashamed] I didn't complete my diary card. You're probably pissed I forgot again. Maybe I shouldn't take up a spot in this therapy anymore.
Intermediate Client Statement 2
[Frustrated] When things get intense, I just act. I don't have any thoughts; I just react.
Intermediate Client Statement 3
[Neutral] I've been trying to cut out my pot use. Every time I stop using, I feel like I'm crawling the walls and just want to use more.
Intermediate Client Statement 4
[Depressed] My life is a mess. I don't think this therapy is helping and I think I need to check into the hospital.
Intermediate Client Statement 5
[Anxious] I got a call from this guy I met 2 weeks ago online, and he said to me last week, "Get your passport and let's go to Jamaica this weekend." I just don't know what to do.

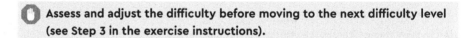 **Assess and adjust the difficulty before moving to the next difficulty level (see Step 3 in the exercise instructions).**

ADVANCED-LEVEL CLIENT STATEMENTS FOR EXERCISE 7
Advanced Client Statement 1
[Ashamed] I'm sorry for leaving you all those messages last week. I thought you were purposely ignoring my calls and just got really upset. When you called me back, I calmed down and felt really guilty about the messages.
Advanced Client Statement 2
[Angry] I'm so pissed today. The shit I've had to deal with this week is unbelievable. I'm just letting you know because I'm in a real mood today, so please don't test me.
Advanced Client Statement 3
[Ashamed] Sometimes I get so frustrated with myself that I hit myself to feel a bit better. I'm feeling so embarrassed even telling you about this.
Advanced Client Statement 4
[Irritated] You're the expert. Why don't you just tell me what you think I should do?
Advanced Client Statement 5
[Angry/hurt] I want to call that stupid girl and yell at her. I want to mess with her. She abandoned me when I needed her.

✋ **Assess and adjust the difficulty here (see Step 3 in the exercise instructions). If appropriate, follow the instructions to make the exercise even more challenging (see Appendix A).**

Example Therapist Responses: Skills Training

Remember: Trainees should attempt to improvise their own responses before reading the example responses. **Do not read the following responses verbatim unless you are having trouble coming up with your own responses!**

EXAMPLE RESPONSES TO BEGINNER-LEVEL CLIENT STATEMENTS FOR EXERCISE 7
Example Response to Beginner Client Statement 1
It sounds like you're having a lot of judgments of yourself. (Criterion 1) Do you notice when you judge yourself harshly that you start feeling more miserable? (Criterion 2) **Option 1:** Would you like some help using mindfulness skills to notice the emotion underneath those judgments? (Criterion 3) **Option 2:** Would you like some help using the STOP skill if that helplessness feeling starts activating urges to act in an unhelpful way? (Criterion 3)
Example Response to Beginner Client Statement 2
It sounds like you're struggling with urges to drink. (Criterion 1) Going to the bar will likely intensify those urges. (Criterion 2) **Option 1:** Would you want some help observing your urges? We could practice noticing when urges come up and then shifting your attention elsewhere, to other things around you in the room. (Criterion 3) **Option 2:** If you ultimately decide to go to the bar, there's a good chance your urges are going to get activated. Would you like help practicing how to use the STOP skill in that situation to interrupt urges to drink? (Criterion 3)
Example Response to Beginner Client Statement 3
It sounds like you're having urges to avoid group sessions because you're having the thought that others are judging you. (Criterion 1) Getting stuck on thoughts that others are judging you is likely contributing to the discomfort you're having in group. (Criterion 2) **Option 1:** I'm wondering if we can work on helping you observe those thoughts and then shift your attention away from them so that you feel more comfortable in group. (Criterion 3) **Option 2:** I'm wondering if we can work on helping you use the STOP skill in moments in group where you are about to act on urges to quit? (Criterion 3)
Example Response to Beginner Client Statement 4
When your mother doesn't respond to you in the way that you want, your anger gets overwhelming and it's hard to control. (Criterion 1) In those moments, when you let yourself go with your anger and yell, you feel relief. However, your relationship with your mom gets worse. (Criterion 2) **Option 1:** During these arguments with your mother, it would be really helpful to use mindfulness skills to observe your anger and to notice when it's starting to get really overwhelming so you can intervene. (Criterion 3) **Option 2:** When you have these strong urges to yell, this would be a perfect moment to use the STOP skill. (Criterion 3)

EXAMPLE RESPONSES TO BEGINNER-LEVEL
CLIENT STATEMENTS FOR EXERCISE 7

Example Response to Beginner Client Statement 5

It sounds like your anger is intense and you've got an urge to make a big decision about your job. (Criterion 1) It sounds like your anger is fueling that urge to act immediately and quit your job. (Criterion 2)

Option 1: Are you willing to try to use mindfulness skills right now to observe and describe the emotions driving your urge to quit right now? (Criterion 3)

Option 2: Are you willing to try the STOP skill to get your emotions down before making any big decision about your job? (Criterion 3)

EXAMPLE RESPONSES TO INTERMEDIATE-LEVEL CLIENT STATEMENTS FOR EXERCISE 7

Example Response to Intermediate Client Statement 1

It sounds like you're having a lot of worry thoughts that I'll judge you. (Criterion 1) These thoughts might get in the way of us figuring out what happened with the diary card. (Criterion 2)

> **Option 1:** Can you see if you can just notice those worry thoughts and shift your attention away from them? (Criterion 3)

> **Option 2:** Are you willing to try the STOP skill to get some space between your emotions and your urge to remove yourself from this treatment? (Criterion 3)

Example Response to Intermediate Client Statement 2

When you experience intense emotions, it's hard to be aware of anything. (Criterion 1) It sounds like when you're in an intense emotional state, it's hard to notice much of what is going on around you, and you act in ways that cause you problems. (Criterion 2)

> **Option 1:** Let's see if we can get you to practice noticing when you're getting sucked into an emotion and instead shift focus to what's going on around you. (Criterion 3)

> **Option 2:** Let's see if we can get you to practice the STOP skill when your emotions start to escalate. (Criterion 3)

Example Response to Intermediate Client Statement 3

You're really struggling with intense urges to use pot. (Criterion 1) Giving in to your urges will make it harder to quit, so it's important that we help you ride out these urges without acting on them. (Criterion 2)

> **Option 1:** I think it would help if you practiced observing your urges, almost like watching your urges as though they are waves flowing onto the beach. (Criterion 3)

> **Option 2:** I think it would help if you practiced using the STOP skill when your urges to use pot increase. (Criterion 3)

Example Response to Intermediate Client Statement 4

It sounds like you're feeling overwhelmed and hopeless right now, and you're having the thought you can't cope. (Criterion 1) While going to the hospital might seem like a solution, it might also reinforce your belief you're not capable of tolerating these big feelings. (Criterion 2)

> **Option 1:** Do you want help mindfully noticing those thoughts and paying attention to the feelings and urges that are coming up without acting on them? (Criterion 3)

> **Option 2:** I think it would be helpful right now to practice the STOP skill, to slow things down so you can make a mindful decision about what you need. (Criterion 3)

Example Response to Intermediate Client Statement 5

You're struggling with a big decision and feel torn about whether to go with this guy. (Criterion 1) Making a big decision like this from an emotional state can make it hard to consider all the consequences. (Criterion 2)

> **Option 1:** I think using mindfulness skills right now might help you take a step back from intense emotion instead of making an impulsive decision. (Criterion 3)

> **Option 2:** The STOP skill might be really helpful right now in giving you some space between your emotions and that intense urge to make a quick decision. (Criterion 3)

EXAMPLE RESPONSES TO ADVANCED-LEVEL CLIENT STATEMENTS FOR EXERCISE 7

Example Response to Advanced Client Statement 1

The challenge for you is that when you get upset, it's hard not to let your behavior follow your mood. (Criterion 1) When you act on these feelings, I know that it gets you into trouble that you later regret. (Criterion 2)

Option 1: This would be a great situation to practice using mindfulness skills. (Criterion 3)

Option 2: This would be a great situation to practice the STOP skill. (Criterion 3)

Example Response to Advanced Client Statement 2

I can see that everything seems like a major hurdle this week. (Criterion 1) I think it would make all the difference to your mood if, when you're having the thought "this is shit," we could help you think about the situation a bit differently. (Criterion 2)

Option 1: Can you use mindfulness skills right now to notice all your judgments and let them go? (Criterion 3)

Option 2: Can you use the STOP skill right now to intervene around your irritation and interrupt urges to lash out at me? (Criterion 3)

Example Response to Advanced Client Statement 3

It is so hard not to act on your urges to harm yourself when your emotions are intense. (Criterion 1) The problem is that acting on urges to harm provides you with relief but makes you feel worse about yourself. (Criterion 2)

Option 1: Let's see if we can help you use mindfulness skills to observe and describe the emotions underlying those self-harm urges. (Criterion 3)

Option 2: Let's see if we can help you use the STOP skill to interrupt the urge to act on self-harm. (Criterion 3)

Example Response to Advanced Client Statement 4

It sounds like I'm coming across in a way that's leaving you thinking that your perspective isn't valuable. (Criterion 1) I can understand why that thought might leave you feeling resentful and like you want to disengage from our session. (Criterion 2)

Option 1: What if instead of disengaging we helped you observe and describe what you're feeling right now and the urges accompanying those feelings? (Criterion 3)

Option 2: What if instead of disengaging we helped you use the STOP skill to interrupt that urge to withdraw? (Criterion 3)

Example Response to Advanced Client Statement 5

It sounds like you're hurt, and it's hard not to want to escape those painful feelings by letting yourself go with your anger. (Criterion 1) I imagine that expressing your anger to this girl will help get rid of some of your pain; at the same time, harassing people is what often destroys your relationships. (Criterion 2)

Option 1: Are you willing to use mindfulness skills right now to observe those painful feelings underneath your anger? (Criterion 3)

Option 2: Are you willing to use the STOP skill right now? If you can use this skill, I think it will be easier to develop the relationships that you want with other people. (Criterion 3)

Modifying Cognitions

Preparations for Exercise 8

1. Read the instructions in Chapter 2.

2. Download the Deliberate Practice Reaction Form and Deliberate Practice Diary Form at https://www.apa.org/pubs/books/deliberate-practice-dialectical-behavior-therapy (see the "Clinician and Practitioner Resources" tab; also available in Appendixes A and B, respectively).

Skill Description

Skill Difficulty Level: Intermediate

One of the primary tasks of a dialectical behavior therapy (DBT) practitioner is to search for and reinforce a client's valid thoughts, interpretations, and beliefs (e.g., through validation strategies). Another task of the DBT therapist is to highlight and address cognitive processes that are contributing to dysfunctional behaviors or maladaptive emotional experiences. By modifying cognitions, DBT therapists help clients observe and change faulty rules governing behavior (e.g., beliefs, underlying assumptions, expectations), nondialectical thinking (e.g., rigid, dichotomous, or extreme thinking), dysfunctional descriptions (e.g., judgments or evaluations), and problematic attentional processes (e.g., rumination). When working with the client to modify cognitions, the therapist's role is to help clients enhance their ability to identify and observe patterns of dysfunctional thinking and to generate functional and accurate thinking and appraisals of situations.

https://doi.org/10.1037/0000322-010

Deliberate Practice in Dialectical Behavior Therapy, by T. Boritz, S. McMain, A. Vaz, and T. Rousmaniere

SKILL CRITERIA FOR EXERCISE 8
1. The therapist highlights the client's problematic or dysfunctional thoughts, assumptions, or beliefs in a nonjudgmental way.
2. The therapist suggests a link between the client's thoughts, assumptions, or beliefs and their maladaptive emotions or behavior.
3. The therapist invites the client to challenge their maladaptive thoughts, assumptions, or beliefs or consider alternative perspectives.

Examples of Modifying Cognitions

Example 1

CLIENT: [*Anxious*] I don't really know anyone who will be at this party. I know I'll be miserable and have a terrible time.

THERAPIST: You're pretty convinced this party will be terrible. (Criterion 1) Since you're having that thought, no wonder you don't want to go. (Criterion 2) Would you like some help interrupting those worry thoughts? (Criterion 3)

Example 2

CLIENT: [*Angry*] My group leader completely dismissed me. She treated me like I was disrupting the group and completely ignored my very legitimate concerns about the mindfulness homework. Screw her—I'm not going back to that group.

THERAPIST: It sounds like you have a lot of assumptions about the therapist's intention toward you. (Criterion 1) Do you notice that this assumption leads you to want to avoid people? (Criterion 2) Do you want some help challenging that assumption? (Criterion 3)

Example 3

CLIENT: [*Sad*] I don't have any friends. I'm such a worthless loser. The world would be better off without me.

THERAPIST: Wow, it seems like your judgments of yourself are pretty strong right now. (Criterion 1) Do you notice that when you're especially judgmental about yourself, it influences your mood, and your thoughts get more extreme? (Criterion 2) Do you want some help letting go of judgments? (Criterion 3)

INSTRUCTIONS FOR EXERCISE 8

Step 1: Role-Play and Feedback

- The client says the first beginner client statement. The therapist improvises a response based on the skill criteria.
- The trainer (or, if not available, the client) provides brief feedback based on the skill criteria.
- The client then repeats the same statement, and the therapist again improvises a response. The trainer (or client) again provides brief feedback.

Step 2: Repeat

- Repeat Step 1 for all the statements at the current difficulty level (beginner, intermediate, or advanced).

Step 3: Assess and Adjust Difficulty

- The therapist completes the Deliberate Practice Reaction Form (see Appendix A) and decides whether to make the exercise easier or harder or to repeat the same difficulty level.

Step 4: Repeat for Approximately 15 Minutes

- Repeat Steps 1 to 3 for at least 15 minutes.
- The trainees then switch therapist and client roles and start over.

➤ **Now it's your turn! Follow Steps 1 and 2 from the instructions.**

Remember: The goal of the role-play is for trainees to practice improvising responses to the client statements in a manner that (a) uses the skill criteria and (b) feels authentic for the trainee. **Example therapist responses for each client statement are provided at the end of this exercise. Trainees should attempt to improvise their own responses before reading the example responses.**

BEGINNER-LEVEL CLIENT STATEMENTS FOR EXERCISE 8
Beginner Client Statement 1
[Sad] I'm a terrible parent. My children would be better off without me.
Beginner Client Statement 2
[Anxious] I know my job interview is going to go poorly; they always do.
Beginner Client Statement 3
[Neutral] I couldn't do the homework. I spent so much time trying to figure out how you wanted me to answer the questions. I got worried I was doing it wrong, so I just stopped.
Beginner Client Statement 4
[Hopeless] I just can't imagine anything changing in my life. It all feels so impossible.
Beginner Client Statement 5
[Irritated] This is stupid. I'm not really sure what we're doing here.

🛑 **Assess and adjust the difficulty before moving to the next difficulty level (see Step 3 in the exercise instructions).**

INTERMEDIATE-LEVEL CLIENT STATEMENTS FOR EXERCISE 8
Intermediate Client Statement 1
[Irritated] I don't need therapy. The problem is with my brain and I just need to find the right medication.
Intermediate Client Statement 2
[Frustrated] I'm just not getting it. I don't understand what you're asking me to do. I'm such an idiot.
Intermediate Client Statement 3
[Ashamed] I was sober for 6 months, but then I drank this weekend. I'm such a failure.
Intermediate Client Statement 4
[Sad] My partner broke up with me today. I know it's stupid that I'm so upset about this; I just really thought we were going to get married.
Intermediate Client Statement 5
[Hopeless] To be honest, I didn't really expect you would really understand me. No therapist ever has.

✋ **Assess and adjust the difficulty before moving to the next difficulty level (see Step 3 in the exercise instructions).**

ADVANCED-LEVEL CLIENT STATEMENTS FOR EXERCISE 8
Advanced Client Statement 1
[Sad] This treatment is my last hope. If it doesn't work, I'm going to kill myself.
Advanced Client Statement 2
[Angry] You don't get it. I can't do these things because I'm depressed. If I wasn't depressed, I could easily do these things and I wouldn't need to be here in the first place.
Advanced Client Statement 3
[Angry] Yeah, I lost my temper at him, but he deserved it. It was his fault for getting me so angry in the first place.
Advanced Client Statement 4
[Irritated] My group leader cut me off while I was trying to share my homework. I don't know why they asked me to share my homework if they didn't want to hear it. I won't make that mistake again. Next time I'll just keep my mouth shut.
Advanced Client Statement 5
[Angry/hurt] I don't understand how you can go on vacation right now. If you cared about me, you would be there for me when I needed you.

> 🖐 **Assess and adjust the difficulty here (see Step 3 in the exercise instructions). If appropriate, follow the instructions to make the exercise even more challenging (see Appendix A).**

Example Therapist Responses: Modifying Cognitions

Remember: Trainees should attempt to improvise their own responses before reading the example responses. **Do not read the following responses verbatim unless you are having trouble coming up with your own responses!**

EXAMPLE RESPONSES TO BEGINNER-LEVEL CLIENT STATEMENTS FOR EXERCISE 8
Example Response to Beginner Client Statement 1
That's a pretty harsh judgment of yourself. (Criterion 1) I can see how that thought might lead you to thinking your children are better off without you and also how that would really intensify your sadness. (Criterion 2) Do you want some help letting go of your judgments? (Criterion 3)
Example Response to Beginner Client Statement 2
You're having a lot of worry thoughts about your interview. (Criterion 1) Do you notice how those worry thoughts are influencing your emotions? (Criterion 2) Do you want some help interrupting those worry thoughts? (Criterion 3)
Example Response to Beginner Client Statement 3
It sounds like you became overwhelmed with judgmental thoughts that you couldn't do your homework correctly. (Criterion 1) It also sounds like those thoughts fueled anxiety and derailed your behavior. (Criterion 2) Do you want some help challenging those thoughts? (Criterion 3)
Example Response to Beginner Client Statement 4
It sounds like you have a deeply held belief that you're powerless to get what you want in your life. (Criterion 1) When you see yourself as powerless, do you notice how it impacts your behavior and urge to give up? (Criterion 2) Would you like some help challenging that thought when it arises? (Criterion 3)
Example Response to Beginner Client Statement 5
Do you notice how your mind suddenly turned to judgmental thoughts about therapy? (Criterion 1) When you have the thought that therapy is stupid, do you notice how it shifts you from what we were discussing? (Criterion 2) Do you want some help letting go of judgments? (Criterion 3)

EXAMPLE RESPONSES TO INTERMEDIATE-LEVEL CLIENT STATEMENTS FOR EXERCISE 8
Example Response to Intermediate Client Statement 1
It sounds like you have the strong belief that you're seriously flawed. (Criterion 1) When you tell yourself that there is something wrong with your brain, do you notice how it impacts your engagement in therapy? (Criterion 2) Do you want some help letting go of judgments? (Criterion 3)
Example Response to Intermediate Client Statement 2
That's a harsh judgment of yourself. (Criterion 1) It sounds like when you start judging yourself, you're a lot less inclined to practice skills. (Criterion 2) Do you want some help interrupting those judgmental thoughts? (Criterion 3)
Example Response to Intermediate Client Statement 3
Do you notice that when you have an alcohol slip, you become very critical of yourself? (Criterion 1) It seems like when you started beating yourself up just now, it had a big impact on your feelings, and your shame intensified. (Criterion 2) Do you want some help reframing those self-critical thoughts? (Criterion 3)
Example Response to Intermediate Client Statement 4
You're understandably really upset, and yet there is a part of you that's telling yourself that it's not OK to have these feelings. (Criterion 1) When you squash these feelings by telling yourself they're unacceptable, I can imagine your sadness feels even more difficult to manage. (Criterion 2) Do you want to try letting go of judgments and accepting any emotions that come up? (Criterion 3)
Example Response to Intermediate Client Statement 5
It sounds like you have a strong belief that you're different from other people and hard to understand. (Criterion 1) Do you notice how that belief affects the way you feel around other people? (Criterion 2) Would you like some help challenging this belief? (Criterion 3)

EXAMPLE RESPONSES TO ADVANCED-LEVEL CLIENT STATEMENTS FOR EXERCISE 8
Example Response to Advanced Client Statement 1
You're thinking that if this therapy doesn't help, this is the end of the road for you. (Criterion 1) I can see how having that perspective would intensify your hopelessness and make it hard to see options other than suicide. (Criterion 2) Do you want some help thinking about this situation a little differently? (Criterion 3)
Example Response to Advanced Client Statement 2
If I had the thought that "I can't do things because I'm depressed," I would find it hard to do anything. (Criterion 1) Do you notice how that thought affects your behavior? (Criterion 2) Would you like some help reframing this thought? (Criterion 3)
Example Response to Advanced Client Statement 3
Do you notice those judgments getting activated? (Criterion 1) It seems like when those judgments start, your anger intensifies and those urges to act on the anger come up—have you noticed that connection? (Criterion 2) Do you want some help letting go of judgments? (Criterion 3)
Example Response to Advanced Client Statement 4
It sounds like in that moment you thought that your group leader wasn't interested in hearing from you. (Criterion 1) I can see how having that assumption might lead you to want to disengage from the group. (Criterion 2) Do you want some help challenging that assumption? (Criterion 3)
Example Response to Advanced Client Statement 5
It sounds like you're thinking that me going on vacation means I don't care about you. (Criterion 1) I can imagine that having that thought brings up a lot of strong feelings. (Criterion 2) Do you want some help thinking about this from a different perspective? (Criterion 3)

Informal Exposure to Emotions

Preparations for Exercise 9

1. Read the instructions in Chapter 2.

2. Download the Deliberate Practice Reaction Form and Deliberate Practice Diary Form at https://www.apa.org/pubs/books/deliberate-practice-dialectical-behavior-therapy (see the "Clinician and Practitioner Resources" tab; also available in Appendixes A and B, respectively).

Skill Description

Skill Difficulty Level: Intermediate

Many clients in dialectical behavior therapy (DBT) experience fear of their emotions and the responses that may accompany them. Clients might fear their emotions due to messages received from the developmental environment discouraging or punishing the experience or expression of certain emotions. Alternatively, some clients may believe nothing good comes from letting oneself feel negative or aversive emotion. As a result, clients may try to avoid them by blocking their experience of them, particularly negative emotions such as shame, anger, fear, guilt, and sadness. When emotional cues are consistently avoided and the experience of emotion inhibited, this reinforces the client's belief that emotions are intolerable and unmanageable. When this occurs, the client loses touch with the adaptive information associated with their primary emotional experience. Additionally, they lose opportunities for learning adaptive coping strategies for expressing and experiencing emotion.

One of the main goals of DBT is to help clients learn to experience, tolerate, and effectively express their emotional needs, without interrupting or blocking the emotions they are feeling. Broadly speaking, informal exposure to emotion helps clients learn to tolerate aversive emotion without escaping or avoiding it. Informal exposure involves

https://doi.org/10.1037/0000322-011
Deliberate Practice in Dialectical Behavior Therapy, by T. Boritz, S. McMain, A. Vaz, and T. Rousmaniere

helping clients understand the principles of exposure and the adaptive function of emotions, focusing the client on their emotions in the here and now and encouraging them to experience their emotions without escape or avoidance. Information exposure can also include helping the client block action tendencies associated with problem emotions (e.g., lashing out when angry, hiding when ashamed, cutting when overwhelmed).

SKILL CRITERIA FOR EXERCISE 9

1. The therapist focuses the client on their emotional experience in the here and now.
2. The therapist validates the client's emotion.
3. The therapist invites the client to stay with and tolerate their emotions (i.e., not to escape or avoid emotions).

Examples of Informal Emotional Exposure

Example 1

CLIENT: [*Guilty*] I've been feeling really guilty about how I've been treating my partner. I don't know if there's anything to do about it, maybe I'm just a jerk.

THERAPIST: It sounds like you're feeling guilty about how you've been treating your partner. (Criterion 1) It makes sense that you're feeling guilty if you think you've done something that's hurt your partner. (Criterion 2) Instead of moving into judging yourself, I wonder if you might try staying with those feelings of guilt. (Criterion 3)

Example 2

CLIENT: [*Ashamed*] Sometimes I get so frustrated with myself that I hit myself to feel a bit better. I'm feeling so embarrassed even telling you about this.

THERAPIST: It sounds like talking to me about your self-harm brings up shame. (Criterion 1) It makes sense you're feeling shame if you're thinking I might judge or reject you. (Criterion 2) Sharing your feelings of embarrassment instead of hiding from them is a great way of decreasing its intensity in the long run. (Criterion 3)

Example 3

CLIENT: [*Sad*] I don't know if I can talk about what happened. I can't talk about it without crying hysterically. I'd rather shut it down and avoid.

THERAPIST: I'm hearing that a lot of sadness gets activated when you talk about what happened, and there's an urge to just push it down and not feel it. (Criterion 1) It makes sense you would want to push those feelings away as the pain is so hard to feel. (Criterion 2) I'm wondering if rather than pushing away from those feelings, you can do the opposite and focus on feeling that sadness? (Criterion 3)

INSTRUCTIONS FOR EXERCISE 9

Step 1: Role-Play and Feedback

- The client says the first beginner client statement. The therapist improvises a response based on the skill criteria.
- The trainer (or, if not available, the client) provides brief feedback based on the skill criteria.
- The client then repeats the same statement, and the therapist again improvises a response. The trainer (or client) again provides brief feedback.

Step 2: Repeat

- Repeat Step 1 for all the statements at the current difficulty level (beginner, intermediate, or advanced).

Step 3: Assess and Adjust Difficulty

- The therapist completes the Deliberate Practice Reaction Form (see Appendix A) and decides whether to make the exercise easier or harder or to repeat the same difficulty level.

Step 4: Repeat for Approximately 15 Minutes

- Repeat Steps 1 to 3 for at least 15 minutes.
- The trainees then switch therapist and client roles and start over.

Now it's your turn! Follow Steps 1 and 2 from the instructions.

Remember: The goal of the role-play is for trainees to practice improvising responses to the client statements in a manner that (a) uses the skill criteria and (b) feels authentic for the trainee. **Example therapist responses for each client statement are provided at the end of this exercise. Trainees should attempt to improvise their own responses before reading the example responses.**

BEGINNER-LEVEL CLIENT STATEMENTS FOR EXERCISE 9
Beginner Client Statement 1
[Sad; looking at the floor and not making eye contact] I'm feeling so depressed. I wasn't even planning on coming to our session.
Beginner Client Statement 2
[Ashamed] I'm feeling so embarrassed right now. I was so anxious before I came to session that I smoked a joint. I just didn't think I could face you sober.
Beginner Client Statement 3
[Angry] I'm so frustrated. I'm trying to tell you about my week, and all you want to hear about it is my diary card.
Beginner Client Statement 4
[Withdrawn] I'm not sure how I'm feeling right now. I just kind of want to get out of here.
Beginner Client Statement 5
[Anxious] I've got a big test coming up tomorrow, and I don't feel prepared. I'm probably going to fail the test and get kicked out of school.

 Assess and adjust the difficulty before moving to the next difficulty level (see Step 3 in the exercise instructions).

INTERMEDIATE-LEVEL CLIENT STATEMENTS FOR EXERCISE 9
Intermediate Client Statement 1
[Ashamed] I didn't complete my diary card. You're probably pissed I forgot again.
Intermediate Client Statement 2
[Frustrated] It feels like you have your agenda and it doesn't matter what I want to talk about.
Intermediate Client Statement 3
[Sad] I'm so lonely. This feeling is unbearable. I have no one in my life I can count on.
Intermediate Client Statement 4
[Anxious] I got a second job interview and I really, really want it. But then I start thinking that nothing I want works out and I shouldn't get my hopes up.
Intermediate Client Statement 5
[Angry] I went to the hospital because I was feeling suicidal and wanted help. They talked to me for, like, 5 minutes then sent me home. What kind of help is that?

 Assess and adjust the difficulty before moving to the next difficulty level (see Step 3 in the exercise instructions).

ADVANCED-LEVEL CLIENT STATEMENTS FOR EXERCISE 9
Advanced Client Statement 1
[Angry] I just don't understand why we need to keep going over this. I thought this treatment was all about people not killing themselves. I drank, I didn't kill myself, can we move on?
Advanced Client Statement 2
[Crying] No one understands what it was like for me last night when I cut myself. Everyone's acting like I didn't even try to use skills.
Advanced Client Statement 3
[Confused] I don't know what I'm feeling. I never really know what I'm feeling. I just know my mind is racing and I feel like I'm going to explode.
Advanced Client Statement 4
[Scared] I can't talk about what happened. I don't even want to think about it. It's too hard. I'm too scared.
Advanced Client Statement 5
[Ashamed] I'm such a piece of shit. If anyone really knew me, they would hate me.

 Assess and adjust the difficulty here (see Step 3 in the exercise instructions). If appropriate, follow the instructions to make the exercise even more challenging (see Appendix A).

Example Therapist Responses: Informal Emotional Exposure

Remember: Trainees should attempt to improvise their own responses before reading the example responses. **Do not read the following responses verbatim unless you are having trouble coming up with your own responses!**

EXAMPLE RESPONSES TO BEGINNER-LEVEL CLIENT STATEMENTS FOR EXERCISE 9
Example Response to Beginner Client Statement 1
I can see you're feeling really sad. (Criterion 1) Sadness can make it hard to feel energy or motivation to do anything. (Criterion 2) Can you stay with your sadness for a moment? There is something important about those feelings that's worth exploring. (Criterion 3)
Example Response to Beginner Client Statement 2
It looks uncomfortable to be feeling so full of shame. (Criterion 1) Shame makes you want to pull away and hide. (Criterion 2) Can you stay with your embarrassment right now and just observe what triggered that emotion? (Criterion 3)
Example Response to Beginner Client Statement 3
You're feeling so frustrated right now. (Criterion 1) If I'm coming across to you like I'm not interested, it's understandable you'd be feeling angry with me. (Criterion 2) If you can shift your mind from the thought "she doesn't care," what other emotions are you aware of feeling right now? (Criterion 3)
Example Response to Beginner Client Statement 4
It sounds like you've got this unclear felt sense of something. (Criterion 1) If that feeling is making you feel upset or uncomfortable, it would make sense you might have the urge to leave the situation that's setting it off. (Criterion 2) Can you try to stay with the feeling instead and see if you can notice any physical sensations in your body? (Criterion 3)
Example Response to Beginner Client Statement 5
It sounds like you're feeling really anxious. (Criterion 1) It would be hard not to feel anxious if you're thinking you're going to fail and get kicked out of school. (Criterion 2) Can you try shifting your attention from your worry thoughts to the emotions underneath them? What emotions get activated when you start thinking about your test? (Criterion 3)

EXAMPLE RESPONSES TO INTERMEDIATE-LEVEL CLIENT STATEMENTS FOR EXERCISE 9
Example Response to Intermediate Client Statement 1
You sound really worried. (Criterion 1) It makes sense you would feel scared if you thought I was going to be angry at you or criticize you for not completing your diary card. (Criterion 2) Can you tell me more about the feelings that are coming up when we start talking about your diary card? (Criterion 3)
Example Response to Intermediate Client Statement 2
I imagine that you may be feeling hurt? (Criterion 1) I'd feel hurt if I thought what I wanted didn't matter to my therapist. (Criterion 2) Can you try to put words to the feelings that are coming up for you? (Criterion 3)
Example Response to Intermediate Client Statement 3
You're feeling so alone. (Criterion 1) This is such a painful feeling, and those ruminative thoughts about having no one in your life only intensify that feeling. (Criterion 2) Can you try to interrupt those thoughts and instead stay with your sadness? (Criterion 3)
Example Response to Intermediate Client Statement 4
It sounds like anxiety is coming up when you start thinking about this job. (Criterion 1) It also sounds like those thoughts about it not working out are a way of getting ahead of potentially feeling disappointed if you don't get the job. (Criterion 2) Can you let go of the thought "nothing will work out" and just notice where in your body you feel any emotional sensations? (Criterion 3)
Example Response to Intermediate Client Statement 5
It sounds like you're feeling really frustrated. (Criterion 1) It's difficult to want more support and not get it. (Criterion 2) Are there any other feelings you're experiencing right now, beneath the anger and frustration? (Criterion 3)

EXAMPLE RESPONSES TO ADVANCED-LEVEL **CLIENT STATEMENTS FOR EXERCISE 9**
Example Response to Advanced Client Statement 1
Talking about your drinking brings up a lot of frustration. (Criterion 1) I can imagine feeling frustrated if I felt like my behavior was being put under the microscope. (Criterion 2) What other emotions come up when we start talking about your drinking? (Criterion 3)
Example Response to Advanced Client Statement 2
It sounds like you're feeling hurt. (Criterion 1) It's painful to feel misunderstood. (Criterion 2) Can you try to stay with that hurt and sadness and put words to those feelings? (Criterion 3)
Example Response to Advanced Client Statement 3
It sounds like everything's feeling mixed up and intense inside right now. (Criterion 1) It's no wonder you're feeling confused if your mind is racing. (Criterion 2) As we help you figure out what you're feeling, can you try to notice any thoughts or sensations in your body right now? (Criterion 3)
Example Response to Advanced Client Statement 4
It sounds like you're feeling terrified. (Criterion 1) It makes sense you would want to turn away from talking about what happened, if you're thinking it's going to make you feel worse. (Criterion 2) Can you pay attention to that scared feeling and try to notice urges that are accompanying it? (Criterion 3)
Example Response to Advanced Client Statement 5
It sounds like shame and disgust are coming up right now. (Criterion 1) If I was having thoughts like "I'm a piece of shit," I might feel shame too and worry about being accepted by others. (Criterion 2) Can you try to let go of your judgments and just pay attention to that feeling of shame and disgust coming up? (Criterion 3)

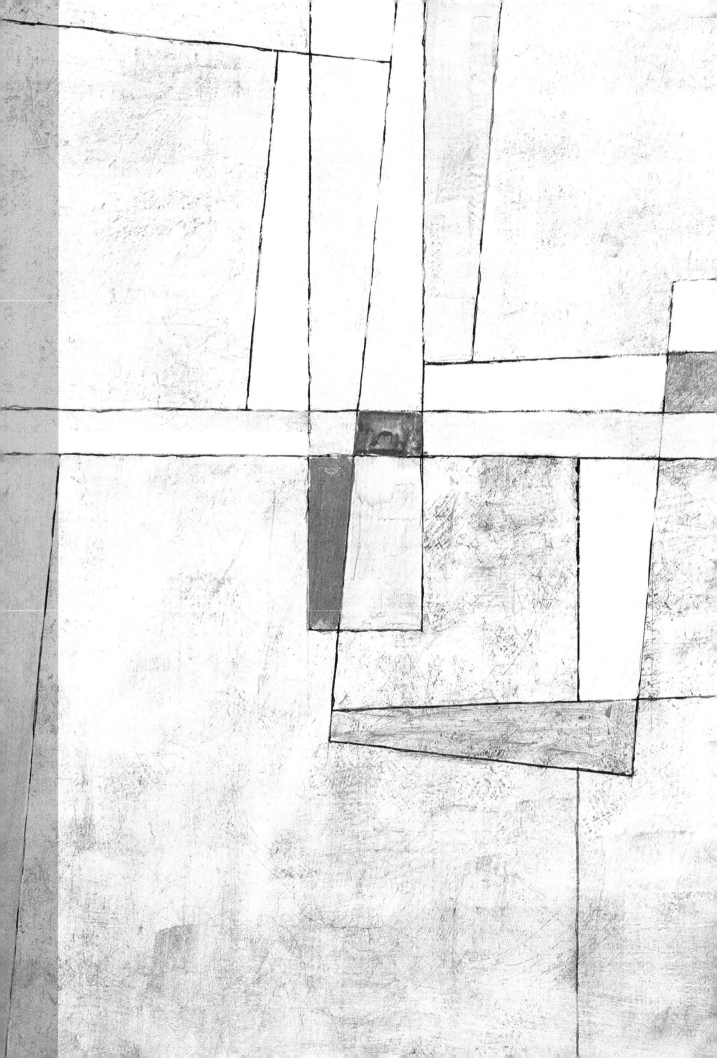

Coaching Clients in Distress

Preparations for Exercise 10

1. Read the instructions in Chapter 2.

2. Download the Deliberate Practice Reaction Form and Deliberate Practice Diary Form at https://www.apa.org/pubs/books/deliberate-practice-dialectical-behavior-therapy (see the "Clinician and Practitioner Resources" tab; also available in Appendixes A and B, respectively).

Skill Description

Skill Difficulty Level: Advanced

We have previously discussed the importance of skills training for helping clients acquire new and more adaptive coping skills for addressing emotion dysregulation and problematic behaviors (see Exercise 7). One context in which skills training can be particularly helpful is in assisting clients in crisis or moments of extreme emotional distress. In these moments, dialectical behavior therapy (DBT) clinicians can coach clients to effectively use distress tolerance skills to down-regulate emotion such that the person is able to refocus their attention and engage in problem solving. When coaching clients in distress, it is important to pay attention to the client's affect rather than the content of the crisis. Validation strategies (Exercise 2) can then be used to reflect the client's emotional responses and their validity. Next, the therapist can encourage the client to use a skill in that moment to tolerate their negative affect without escaping it via problematic behaviors or secondary emotions. While validation on its own can contribute to a decrease in the intensity of painful emotions, coaching clients to use skills provides additional instruction on strategies that can be used in future crisis situations.

Although there is a range of DBT skills that can be used when coaching clients in distress, for the purposes of this exercise, we focus on distress-tolerance TIPP skills: temperature, intense exercise, paced breathing, and paired muscle relaxation. TIPP skills

https://doi.org/10.1037/0000322-012

Deliberate Practice in Dialectical Behavior Therapy, by T. Boritz, S. McMain, A. Vaz, and T. Rousmaniere

are used when a person is in crisis or in a moment of high distress. These skills are intended to bring down the intensity of an emotion to a level where the client is able to cope with difficult situations and feelings more effectively. The TIPP skills have the effect of rapidly changing biological response patterns, leading to a reduction in emotional arousal. *Temperature* involves changing the temperature of your face using cold water or ice while holding your breath (e.g., dunking your head in a bowl of ice-cold water, putting an ice pack or cold compress on your face, splashing cold water on your face). This induces the human dive reflex, which slows down your heart rate and reduces physiological and emotional arousal very quickly. *Intense exercise* involves engaging in a high-intensity workout to help your body get rid of the negative energy that can sometimes be stored from strong emotions. Intense exercise also leads to the natural release of endorphins, which can help combat any negative emotions such as anger, anxiety, or sadness. Intense exercise can include running, walking at a fast pace, or doing jumping jacks. *Paced breathing* helps the body relax by slowing down inhalations and exhalations. Our bodies naturally relax when we breathe out, so if we can slow our breathing down and breathe out for longer than we breathe in then we will start to relax. *Paired muscle relaxation* involves deep breathing while slowly tensing each body muscle group then relaxing.

SKILL CRITERIA FOR EXERCISE 10

1. The therapist validates the client's affect and/or the difficulty of tolerating affect.
2. The therapist invites or instructs the client to use a distress tolerance TIPP skill (i.e., temperature, intensive exercise, paced breathing, or paired muscle relaxation) to reduce the intensity of emotional distress.

Examples of Coaching Clients in Distress

Example 1

CLIENT: [*Intense anger*] I'm so angry at my boss. I just want to quit my job.

THERAPIST: Your anger is really intense, and your impulse is to do something abrupt like quit work. (Criterion 1) I'm wondering if we can do some paced breathing together right now to bring your anger down, so we can then think together about whether quitting work is the most effective decision. (Criterion 2)

Example 2

CLIENT: [*Distressed*] I don't know what I'm going to do. I'm in so much debt, my parents are going to kill me when they find out.

THERAPIST: You sound really worried. (Criterion 1) I'm wondering if you want to grab an ice pack right now and put it on your face? It might help you bring your anxiety down so we can figure out how to help you address this problem. (Criterion 2)

Example 3

CLIENT: [*Suddenly appears tuned out*] It's hard for me to think clearly right now. I think I'm beginning to dissociate.

THERAPIST: You look like you're getting emotionally overwhelmed right now and I can see it's hard to focus. (Criterion 1) Can we help you be more present? I'm wondering if doing some jumping jacks may help reduce your intense emotions? (Criterion 2)

INSTRUCTIONS FOR EXERCISE 10

Step 1: Role-Play and Feedback

- The client says the first beginner client statement. The therapist improvises a response based on the skill criteria.
- The trainer (or, if not available, the client) provides brief feedback based on the skill criteria.
- The client then repeats the same statement, and the therapist again improvises a response. The trainer (or client) again provides brief feedback.

Step 2: Repeat

- Repeat Step 1 for all the statements at the current difficulty level (beginner, intermediate, or advanced).

Step 3: Assess and Adjust Difficulty

- The therapist completes the Deliberate Practice Reaction Form (see Appendix A) and decides whether to make the exercise easier or harder or to repeat the same difficulty level.

Step 4: Repeat for Approximately 15 Minutes

- Repeat Steps 1 to 3 for at least 15 minutes.
- The trainees then switch therapist and client roles and start over.

> **Now it's your turn! Follow Steps 1 and 2 from the instructions.**

Remember: The goal of the role-play is for trainees to practice improvising responses to the client statements in a manner that (a) uses the skill criteria and (b) feels authentic for the trainee. **Example therapist responses for each client statement are provided at the end of this exercise. Trainees should attempt to improvise their own responses before reading the example responses.**

BEGINNER-LEVEL CLIENT STATEMENTS FOR EXERCISE 10
Beginner Client Statement 1
[Crying] I'm such a loser. I screw up everything. I don't know why I'm even trying anymore.
Beginner Client Statement 2
[Withdrawn] I don't really know what to say right now. I can't even really remember what you just asked me. I think I'm beginning to dissociate.
Beginner Client Statement 3
[Depressed] I just can't cope with my life right now. Everything is getting worse, and I don't think this therapy is helping. Maybe I need to go back to the inpatient unit.
Beginner Client Statement 4
[Anxious] My landlord just called and told me if I don't pay my rent today, he's going to evict me. I don't know what to do. What should I do? I'm in so much trouble.
Beginner Client Statement 5
[Ashamed] I tried using skills, but this week was just too hard. It's just too much. I can't live like this. I don't want to be here anymore.

 Assess and adjust the difficulty before moving to the next difficulty level (see Step 3 in the exercise instructions).

INTERMEDIATE-LEVEL CLIENT STATEMENTS FOR EXERCISE 10
Intermediate Client Statement 1
[Distressed] I'm just so overwhelmed right now. I can't even think clearly.
Intermediate Client Statement 2
[Angry] One of my group members was just sitting in the corner on her phone. It was so disrespectful. Why would you even come to group if you're not going to participate? It's so rude. I'm so pissed I can't even think about our session.
Intermediate Client Statement 3
[Sad, crying] I feel like no one in my life is here for me. I'm so alone. No one would miss me if I was gone.
Intermediate Client Statement 4
[Ashamed] I'm so humiliated. I can't even look at you right now. I'm a horrible person.
Intermediate Client Statement 5
[Anxious] I feel like I'm having a panic attack. I can't breathe.

 Assess and adjust the difficulty before moving to the next difficulty level (see Step 3 in the exercise instructions).

ADVANCED-LEVEL CLIENT STATEMENTS FOR EXERCISE 10
Advanced Client Statement 1
[Angry] My psychiatrist is such a jerk. She won't give me more pain meds even though I can barely function right now. I'm so close to going back to her office and telling her exactly what I think of her.
Advanced Client Statement 2
[Crying and hyperventilating] I can't deal with this anymore. I'm done trying. I've got to get out of this office.
Advanced Client Statement 3
[Crying] I'm such a burden, everyone would be better off without me. You would probably be so relieved if I killed myself and you didn't have to deal with me anymore.
Advanced Client Statement 4
[Withdrawn] I'm having really strong urges to self-harm. I've been fighting them all week, but they're just getting stronger. Nothing else is helping and I need some relief.
Advanced Client Statement 5
[Yelling] You're just like the rest of them. No therapist has ever helped me. Everyone just wants to change me. No one actually wants to help me.

Assess and adjust the difficulty here (see Step 3 in the exercise instructions). If appropriate, follow the instructions to make the exercise even more challenging (see Appendix A).

Example Therapist Responses: Coaching Clients in Distress

Remember: Trainees should attempt to improvise their own responses before reading the example responses. **Do not read the following responses verbatim unless you are having trouble coming up with your own responses!**

EXAMPLE RESPONSES TO BEGINNER-LEVEL CLIENT STATEMENTS FOR EXERCISE 10
Example Response to Beginner Client Statement 1
It sounds like you're judging yourself pretty harshly and feeling hopeless right now. (Criterion 1) Would you be willing to do some paced breathing to see if we can get those emotions down to a more manageable level? (Criterion 2)
Example Response to Beginner Client Statement 2
It looks like you're having some difficulty concentrating right now. (Criterion 1) Now might be a perfect time to get an ice pack and put it on your face to see if that helps refocus. (Criterion 2)
Example Response to Beginner Client Statement 3
You're feeling overwhelmed, and it's understandable that you want to feel better. (Criterion 1) Would you like my help bringing down that feeling of overwhelm right now? Doing some paced breathing right now might help take the edge off of your distress. (Criterion 2)
Example Response to Beginner Client Statement 4
I think that getting news like that would make anyone feel anxious! (Criterion 1) Why don't we do some paced breathing together right now to help bring down your distress so we can do some problem solving together? (Criterion 2)
Example Response to Beginner Client Statement 5
It sounds like you're feeling overwhelmed and hopeless right now and looking for a way to escape that feeling. (Criterion 1) Why don't we try doing some paired muscle relaxation? It's possible that will help bring a bit of relief to those feelings right now. (Criterion 2)

EXAMPLE RESPONSES TO INTERMEDIATE-LEVEL CLIENT STATEMENTS FOR EXERCISE 10
Example Response to Intermediate Client Statement 1
It can be really hard to think clearly when emotions are high. (Criterion 1) Why don't we do 10 jumping jacks together and see if that helps get your distress down? (Criterion 2)
Example Response to Intermediate Client Statement 2
I imagine getting really distracted by this person and feeling frustrated by that. (Criterion 1) I'm wondering if it may help to do some paired muscle relaxation right now to bring your tension down? (Criterion 2)
Example Response to Intermediate Client Statement 3
It sounds like you're feeling really sad and alone right now, and these feelings are painful and hard to bear. (Criterion 1) I want to hear more about what set off those feelings, but I think it might be helpful to first do some paced breathing together to help decrease the intensity of those emotions. Are you willing to do some breathing with me? (Criterion 2)
Example Response to Intermediate Client Statement 4
When shame is really high, it often comes with the urge to hide or turn away from others or do anything to escape the discomfort of feeling judged or rejected. (Criterion 1) I wonder if instead of avoiding these feelings, you might grab an ice pack and practice some deep breathing to try to take the edge off of your intense feelings? (Criterion 2)
Example Response to Intermediate Client Statement 5
Your anxiety is getting really high right now, and it looks difficult to breathe. (Criterion 1) Let's do some paced breathing together to see if we can bring your anxiety down a bit. (Criterion 2)

EXAMPLE RESPONSES TO ADVANCED-LEVEL CLIENT STATEMENTS FOR EXERCISE 10

Example Response to Advanced Client Statement 1

It sounds like you're feeling angry and frustrated right now and you want to lash out at your psychiatrist. While that might help bring some relief in the moment, it might also have some negative consequences. (Criterion 1) Do you want to try instead to get your anger down so you can make a mindful decision about how to communicate with your psychiatrist? Would you be willing to use an ice pack to try to decrease your anger? (Criterion 2)

Example Response to Advanced Client Statement 2

I can see how distressed you're feeling right now, and it makes total sense to me you would want to try to get rid of that feeling. (Criterion 1) Would you be willing to engage in some intense exercise? We could run up and down the stairs a couple of times to see if that helps bring down the intensity of that feeling of overwhelm? (Criterion 2)

Example Response to Advanced Client Statement 3

You're in a lot of pain right now and thinking you're a burden to others. (Criterion 1) When pain is really high, like it is for you now, it can be helpful to shift the intensity of those emotions. Would you be willing to fill the sink with really cold water and dunk your face in it a few times? It might help reduce the intensity to a more manageable level so we can talk more about how you're feeling. (Criterion 2)

Example Response to Advanced Client Statement 4

It makes perfect sense to me that you would want some relief at this moment, and self-harm works in the short term to bring down intense emotions. (Criterion 1) One thought I'm having is we might try to do some paired muscle relaxation together to see if that brings some of the relief you're seeking. (Criterion 2)

Example Response to Advanced Client Statement 5

I'd feel angry too if I felt like I wasn't being helped. (Criterion 1) I'd like to try to understand better what help you're wanting right now, but it's going to be hard to do that if you're feeling really dysregulated. Would you be willing to do some paced breathing with me for a few minutes to see if that brings down the intensity of your anger so we can try to figure this out together? (Criterion 2)

Promoting Dialectical Thinking Through Both–And Statements

Preparations for Exercise 11

1. Read the instructions in Chapter 2.

2. Download the Deliberate Practice Reaction Form and Deliberate Practice Diary Form at https://www.apa.org/pubs/books/deliberate-practice-dialectical-behavior-therapy (see the "Clinician and Practitioner Resources" tab; also available in Appendixes A and B, respectively).

Skill Description

Skill Difficulty Level: Advanced

One of the primary goals of dialectical behavior therapy (DBT) is to increase dialectical thinking and to help clients shift typically extreme emotions and behaviors to more balanced, effective responses. In DBT, the therapist pushes for change in the client while helping the client accept their emotional experience and those aspects of their reality that cannot be changed. One way that DBT therapists support their clients in this endeavor is by using dialectical strategies to balance problem-solving solutions that are oriented toward change with acceptance-focused solutions that are oriented toward helping clients tolerate reality as it is (Sayrs & Linehan, 2019). These two seemingly opposing positions are balanced through the adoption of a dialectical stance (i.e., embraces the view that therapists can simultaneously hold the positions of accepting the client as they are and moving them toward change) as well as through a set of dialectical communication strategies. When taking a dialectical approach, validation and change strategies are woven together so that both are conveyed in communication with the client.

When the therapist identifies rigid or extreme thinking (i.e., nondialectical thinking), they highlight how both sides of an issue can be true. For example, a client may use substances to help escape distressing flashbacks of past traumatic events. The validity of this behavior is that it solves the problem of ending or numbing aversive experiences. On the other hand, substance use creates other problems for the client that further exacerbate their pain and suffering. In this scenario, the therapist may use dialectical communication to highlight to the client that it makes sense they want to escape painful emotions in the moment and that they need to develop skills for effectively managing flashbacks to decrease pain over the long run. For this exercise, we focus on using "both-and" language to reframe polarizing or extreme statements or to highlight seemingly opposed parts of a client statement that are equally true and valid.

SKILL CRITERION FOR EXERCISE 11

1. The therapist balances use of acceptance-oriented strategies with change-oriented strategies through both–and statements.

Examples of Promoting Dialectical Thinking Through Both–And Statements

Example 1

CLIENT: [*Sad*] Things are just so hard right now. I'm coming to therapy, trying to make these big changes, but I'm struggling day to day.

THERAPIST: You are working really hard to get better, and it's really difficult.

Example 2

CLIENT: [*Frustrated*] I can't believe you're going on vacation next week. You won't be there for me if I need you.

THERAPIST: Yes, it would be better for you if I were not going away next week and it's OK that I'm going away next week.

Example 3

CLIENT: [*Ashamed*] If you understood how much pain I'm in, you wouldn't ask me to stop cutting. Cutting is the only relief I can get right now.

THERAPIST: Cutting brings you relief and it maintains your pain in the long run.

INSTRUCTIONS FOR EXERCISE 11

Step 1: Role-Play and Feedback

- The client says the first beginner client statement. The therapist improvises a response based on the skill criteria.
- The trainer (or, if not available, the client) provides brief feedback based on the skill criteria.
- The client then repeats the same statement, and the therapist again improvises a response. The trainer (or client) again provides brief feedback.

Step 2: Repeat

- Repeat Step 1 for all the statements at the current difficulty level (beginner, intermediate, or advanced).

Step 3: Assess and Adjust Difficulty

- The therapist completes the Deliberate Practice Reaction Form (see Appendix A) and decides whether to make the exercise easier or harder or to repeat the same difficulty level.

Step 4: Repeat for Approximately 15 Minutes

- Repeat Steps 1 to 3 for at least 15 minutes.
- The trainees then switch therapist and client roles and start over.

> **Now it's your turn! Follow Steps 1 and 2 from the instructions.**

Remember: The goal of the role-play is for trainees to practice improvising responses to the client statements in a manner that (a) uses the skill criteria and (b) feels authentic for the trainee. **Example therapist responses for each client statement are provided at the end of this exercise. Trainees should attempt to improvise their own responses before reading the example responses.**

BEGINNER-LEVEL CLIENT STATEMENTS FOR EXERCISE 11
Beginner Client Statement 1
[Sad] I'm so confused. I want this relationship to work so badly, but things between me and my partner are so difficult right now. Every time we're around each other, we get into these huge fights. I love them so much but being together right now isn't working.
Beginner Client Statement 2
[Anxious] I feel so nervous all the time. Things are going well for the first time in my life. I've made so many changes and I can see all the positive effects, but I keep waiting for the other shoe to drop.
Beginner Client Statement 3
[Irritated] I'm trying so hard. I don't think you understand how hard it is. Some days I just don't feel like working so hard.
Beginner Client Statement 4
[Ashamed] I did what we talked about. I texted my friend when I was feeling down last night, but she didn't respond. I felt really upset at the time but was able to validate my emotions.
Beginner Client Statement 5
[Ashamed] I'm sorry for leaving the session so abruptly last week. I felt like you were judging me, and I just needed to take some space to calm down. I didn't mean it when I told you I thought you were a bad therapist.

 Assess and adjust the difficulty before moving to the next difficulty level (see Step 3 in the exercise instructions).

INTERMEDIATE-LEVEL CLIENT STATEMENTS FOR EXERCISE 11
Intermediate Client Statement 1
[Frustrated] You don't get it—I'd use skills if I could, but when I get anxious, I go from zero to 100. There's no time to use skills!
Intermediate Client Statement 2
[Sad] I want to leave my job, but I don't want to disappoint my boss. He's been really supportive. I feel like if I leave, I'm going to let him down.
Intermediate Client Statement 3
[Confused] My friend keeps asking for my help. She's suicidal and in constant crisis and needs so much support. I guess because we're both in DBT I can kind of help her figure out which skills to use. I want to be there for her, but it can get pretty overwhelming sometimes and trigger my own suicide urges.
Intermediate Client Statement 4
[Withdrawn] This is too hard. Talking about this stuff brings up too many bad memories.
Intermediate Client Statement 5
[Frustrated] I had a tough week. My parents were driving me crazy and then I got into a fight with my sister because she took their side. I tried to use the skills we were learning in group but couldn't figure out which ones to use. I thought about calling you but thought I should be able to figure it out by myself and didn't want to bother you.

 Assess and adjust the difficulty before moving to the next difficulty level (see Step 3 in the exercise instructions).

ADVANCED-LEVEL CLIENT STATEMENTS FOR EXERCISE 11
Advanced Client Statement 1
[Angry] My mom just wouldn't stop nagging me. I asked her to leave me alone, but she just kept going. So I got really in her face and screamed at her. I think I scared her. She backed off.
Advanced Client Statement 2
[Anxious] I don't really know where to start. I feel like I can't do anything right. I missed group this week because I was too anxious to face everyone. And I'm still feeling anxious right now. Maybe I should cancel group again today.
Advanced Client Statement 3
[Angry] You make me feel like I'm the problem. We always focus on what I did wrong or what I could do differently, but what about everyone else and their shitty behavior?
Advanced Client Statement 4
[Guilty] I feel like I should spend the holidays with my family. I know they want to see me, and they're so great in so many ways. But when I go home, my family constantly misgenders me, and I leave feeling depressed and even more disconnected.
Advanced Client Statement 5
[Angry] This is bullshit! I told you what the problem is and you just don't want to help me. You don't give a shit about me.

 Assess and adjust the difficulty here (see Step 3 in the exercise instructions). If appropriate, follow the instructions to make the exercise even more challenging (see Appendix A).

Example Therapist Responses: Promoting Dialectical Thinking Through Both–And Statements

Remember: Trainees should attempt to improvise their own responses before reading the example responses. **Do not read the following responses verbatim unless you are having trouble coming up with your own responses!**

EXAMPLE RESPONSES TO BEGINNER-LEVEL CLIENT STATEMENTS FOR EXERCISE 11
Example Response to Beginner Client Statement 1
You love him, and you need to take a break from him right now.
Example Response to Beginner Client Statement 2
You're proud of the changes you've made, and you're feeling scared about what comes next.
Example Response to Beginner Client Statement 3
You are doing your best, and you need to try harder.
Example Response to Beginner Client Statement 4
You were disappointed by the situation, and you accepted it for what it was.
Example Response to Beginner Client Statement 5
You really hurt my feelings, and we will work it out.

EXAMPLE RESPONSES TO INTERMEDIATE-LEVEL CLIENT STATEMENTS FOR EXERCISE 11
Example Response to Intermediate Client Statement 1
It's hard to use skills when emotions are so high, and it's the perfect time to use them.
Example Response to Intermediate Client Statement 2
You care about your boss, and you don't want to continue in the job.
Example Response to Intermediate Client Statement 3
Someone may have good reasons for wanting something from you, and you may have good reasons for saying "no" or observing your limits.
Example Response to Intermediate Client Statement 4
It's incredibly painful and not to avoid these feelings when they come up is necessary to reduce them in the long run.
Example Response to Intermediate Client Statement 5
You can try to figure out a solution on your own, and sometimes you need help and support from others.

EXAMPLE RESPONSES TO ADVANCED-LEVEL CLIENT STATEMENTS FOR EXERCISE 11
Example Response to Advanced Client Statement 1
Screaming at your mom helped get her to back off, and there are probably more effective strategies for achieving that goal.
Example Response to Advanced Client Statement 2
Avoiding group relieves your anxiety in the short term, and learning how to feel anxious without needing to escape it is the very thing that's going to help you decrease your anxiety in the long term.
Example Response to Advanced Client Statement 3
You want to get a handle on your behavior, and you want to acknowledge the impact other people's behaviors has had on you.
Example Response to Advanced Client Statement 4
You appreciate their good qualities, and you want to limit how much time you spend with them because it's hurtful when they misgender you.
Example Response to Advanced Client Statement 5
I can care about you and refuse to do something you ask.

Responding to Suicidal Ideation

Preparations for Exercise 12

1. Read the instructions in Chapter 2.

2. Download the Deliberate Practice Reaction Form and Deliberate Practice Diary Form at https://www.apa.org/pubs/books/deliberate-practice-dialectical-behavior-therapy (see the "Clinician and Practitioner Resources" tab; also available in Appendixes A and B, respectively).

Skill Description

Skill Difficulty Level: Advanced

Many people who are struggling with severe emotion dysregulation may engage in self-harm and suicidal behavior. The treatment of individuals with suicidal behaviors requires a structured protocol to guide response. For the purposes of this exercise, we will be focusing on how to respond specifically to suicidal ideation (i.e., thoughts of death, urges to die).

For many clients, suicidal ideation often occurs in contexts where psychological pain feels unbearable or never ending. In such circumstances, suicide can be understood as a desire to avoid or end "intolerable, unendurable, unacceptable anguish" (Shneidman, 1992, p. 54). Therefore, one essential therapeutic task is to assess and highlight the emotion pain or problem that is driving a client's suicidal thoughts. Once the therapist has identified the emotional problem that is driving the client's suicidal thoughts, they should next discuss alternative solutions to the problematic situation. This may include tolerating the painful emotion they are experiencing (e.g., using distress tolerance skills) or using problem-solving skills to address the situation (e.g., via solution analysis).

https://doi.org/10.1037/0000322-014
Deliberate Practice in Dialectical Behavior Therapy, by T. Boritz, S. McMain, A. Vaz, and T. Rousmaniere

It is essential to note here that how a therapist responds to any single instance of a suicidal behavior should always be informed by information about the client's risk history, the client's case formulation, their specific context and situation, and the therapeutic relationship. At all stages of training, supervision and consultation should be sought when determining how best to respond and intervene if your client expresses suicidal ideation or discloses suicidal behavior.

SKILL CRITERIA FOR EXERCISE 12

1. The therapist highlights the client's distressing emotion.
2. The therapist links the client's emotion with urges to escape, avoid, or find relief from their distress through suicidal thoughts.
3. The therapist helps the client consider more effective ways to solve the emotional problem driving their suicidal thoughts.

Examples of Responding to Suicidal Ideation

Example 1

CLIENT: [*Ashamed*] I tried using skills, but this week it was just too hard. It's just too much. I can't live like this.

THERAPIST: It sounds like you're feeling overwhelmed. (Criterion 1) Suicide seems like the only way to manage these feelings. (Criterion 2) Although suicide may seem like the only solution, I'm thinking we can find a more effective way of helping you manage your distressing feelings right now. (Criterion 3)

Example 2

CLIENT: [*Sad*] I don't have any friends. I have nobody. I really want to just kill myself.

THERAPIST: It sounds like you're really struggling with some overwhelming feelings of aloneness (Criterion 1) and that your brain is going toward thoughts of suicide to cope with these feelings. (Criterion 2) I'm wondering if you want my help figuring out other ways to help you feel less alone? (Criterion 3)

Example 3

CLIENT: [*Withdrawn*] I'm just feeling done with everything. Everything's a battle, and I'm exhausted. I want to give up and end it—I need a break.

THERAPIST: You sound emotionally exhausted. (Criterion 1) It sounds like the real issue underlying your thoughts of suicide is a desire to find relief from these feelings. (Criterion 2) I know that this is hard, and I want to help you find some alternative ways of finding some relief right now. (Criterion 3)

INSTRUCTIONS FOR EXERCISE 12

Step 1: Role-Play and Feedback

- The client says the first beginner client statement. The therapist improvises a response based on the skill criteria.
- The trainer (or, if not available, the client) provides brief feedback based on the skill criteria.
- The client then repeats the same statement, and the therapist again improvises a response. The trainer (or client) again provides brief feedback.

Step 2: Repeat

- Repeat Step 1 for all the statements at the current difficulty level (beginner, intermediate, or advanced).

Step 3: Assess and Adjust Difficulty

- The therapist completes the Deliberate Practice Reaction Form (see Appendix A) and decides whether to make the exercise easier or harder or to repeat the same difficulty level.

Step 4: Repeat for Approximately 15 Minutes

- Repeat Steps 1 to 3 for at least 15 minutes.
- The trainees then switch therapist and client roles and start over.

Now it's your turn! Follow Steps 1 and 2 from the instructions.

Remember: The goal of the role-play is for trainees to practice improvising responses to the client statements in a manner that (a) uses the skill criteria and (b) feels authentic for the trainee. **Example therapist responses for each client statement are provided at the end of this exercise. Trainees should attempt to improvise their own responses before reading the example responses.**

BEGINNER-LEVEL CLIENT STATEMENTS FOR EXERCISE 12
Beginner Client Statement 1
[Ashamed] I think about dying all the time. I feel relief when I think about ending this painful existence.
Beginner Client Statement 2
[Depressed] I'm feeling so depressed today and wasn't even planning on coming to our session. I just want to die.
Beginner Client Statement 3
[Agitated] I feel like such a failure . . . I can't get a job, I can't find a partner. Everything is terrible and I'm such a loser. I try to not let it get to me, but I'm beginning to feel like I can't handle anything in this life.
Beginner Client Statement 4
[Anxious] I keep having panic attacks. I feel like I'm going crazy. I can't live like this. Sometimes I think it might be easier to kill myself than to feel like this all the time.
Beginner Client Statement 5
[Crying] My boyfriend dumped me last night. It was so humiliating. I really thought we were going to spend our lives together. I don't know what there is to live for anymore.

🛑 **Assess and adjust the difficulty before moving to the next difficulty level (see Step 3 in the exercise instructions).**

INTERMEDIATE-LEVEL CLIENT STATEMENTS FOR EXERCISE 12
Intermediate Client Statement 1
[Crying] I'm such a burden; everyone would be better off without me.
Intermediate Client Statement 2
[Ashamed] I tried using skills, but I felt suicidal all week. I tried to distract myself, but the thoughts kept coming. It's just too much. I can't live like this.
Intermediate Client Statement 3
[Crying and hyperventilating] I can't deal with this anymore. I'm done trying.
Intermediate Client Statement 4
[Sad] I'm a terrible mother. My children would be better off without me.
Intermediate Client Statement 5
[Hopeless] I just can't imagine anything changing in my life. It all feels so impossible. Most of the time, I just think I'd rather be dead than keep trying to no effect.

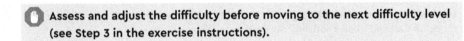 **Assess and adjust the difficulty before moving to the next difficulty level (see Step 3 in the exercise instructions).**

ADVANCED-LEVEL CLIENT STATEMENTS FOR EXERCISE 12
Advanced Client Statement 1
[Angry] I'm telling you I'm suicidal and you're telling me to grab an ice pack. I'm telling you I have no reasons left to live. How is an ice pack going to help me with that?
Advanced Client Statement 2
[Sad] I keep relapsing. Every time I get sober, I think this time it's going to stick. And then it doesn't. I'm just letting everyone down. I can't handle their disappointment. The world would be a better place if I took myself out of it.
Advanced Client Statement 3
[Ashamed] If people knew who I really was inside. If they knew the things I did . . . It's just a matter of time until they realize. I can't bear it. I think sometimes I should kill myself before they find out I'm a monster.
Advanced Client Statement 4
[Sad] Once this session ends, I don't know what I'll do. I don't think I can cope.
Advanced Client Statement 5
[Anxious] Nighttime is the worst. I feel so alone and there's no one to call. The suicidal thoughts start and there's nothing I can do to stop them.

> **Assess and adjust the difficulty here (see Step 3 in the exercise instructions). If appropriate, follow the instructions to make the exercise even more challenging (see Appendix A).**

Example Therapist Responses: Responding to Suicidal Ideation

Remember: Trainees should attempt to improvise their own responses before reading the example responses. **Do not read the following responses verbatim unless you are having trouble coming up with your own responses!**

EXAMPLE RESPONSES TO BEGINNER-LEVEL CLIENT STATEMENTS FOR EXERCISE 12
Example Response to Beginner Client Statement 1
You're in a lot of pain right now. (Criterion 1) When you think about suicide, it brings some relief because you are imagining an end to that pain. (Criterion 2) Can we work together on finding more helpful ways to find relief from your pain? (Criterion 3)
Example Response to Beginner Client Statement 2
You're struggling right now and feeling really down and depressed. (Criterion 1) Your brain is going to thoughts of suicide as a solution to your current state. (Criterion 2) Can we help you get your brain away from these thoughts and understand how you're feeling and how to solve what's really bothering you? (Criterion 3)
Example Response to Beginner Client Statement 3
You're upset with yourself and feeling a lot of shame. (Criterion 1) When you're feeling this way, it's hard not to have thoughts that you can't cope with your life. (Criterion 2) I'm wondering if we can help you shift your attention away from thoughts that you can't cope and focus instead on how to help you feel more capable? (Criterion 3)
Example Response to Beginner Client Statement 4
As I'm listening to you, I can feel your terror and your sense of being out of control. (Criterion 1) The thoughts of suicide seem like a way to escape these feelings. (Criterion 2) Can we look at other ways of helping you feel more comfortable and address what you really need right now to feel more in control? (Criterion 3)
Example Response to Beginner Client Statement 5
You're feeling rejected and alone. (Criterion 1) When you feel this way, your mind starts telling you there's no point in living. (Criterion 2) I'm wondering if we can help you figure out how to manage that feeling of loneliness and cope with the breakup? (Criterion 3)

EXAMPLE RESPONSES TO INTERMEDIATE-LEVEL CLIENT STATEMENTS FOR EXERCISE 12
Example Response to Intermediate Client Statement 1
You're feeling a lot of sadness and guilt. (Criterion 1) Right now, all you can think is that you're such a burden and the solution is to die. (Criterion 2) I'm wondering if we can help you find some more effective ways to address how you're feeling? (Criterion 3)
Example Response to Intermediate Client Statement 2
It sounds like you're feeling overwhelmed. (Criterion 1) When you're in this overwhelmed state, it's hard to get your mind off thoughts of suicide as a way of bringing relief to this feeling. (Criterion 2) Can we help you shift your attention away from thoughts of suicide and try to understand how to address what's really bothering you? (Criterion 3)
Example Response to Intermediate Client Statement 3
You sound exhausted and hopeless. (Criterion 1) You've been trying so hard, and suicide seems like the only way out. (Criterion 2) There is never just one solution; even though it's so hard, if you keep trying and don't give up, we can work together to find some more helpful ways to cope with your emotions. (Criterion 3)
Example Response to Intermediate Client Statement 4
You sound overwhelmed with feelings of disappointment and guilt. (Criterion 1) When you're in such pain, it's hard not to tell yourself that killing yourself is the best solution to the problem. (Criterion 2) I'm wondering if we can find other ways to help you manage those feelings? (Criterion 3)
Example Response to Intermediate Client Statement 5
You're feeling overwhelmed and hopeless. (Criterion 1) When you're got this hopeless feeling, the thought of death feels like a relief. (Criterion 2) I'm wondering if we can help you find some other ways to find comfort right now? (Criterion 3)

EXAMPLE RESPONSES TO ADVANCED-LEVEL CLIENT STATEMENTS FOR EXERCISE 12
Example Response to Advanced Client Statement 1
Underneath your frustration it sounds like you're feeling alone and afraid you're not getting the support you need. (Criterion 1) When you're feeling alone and afraid, your brain goes to thoughts of suicide. (Criterion 2) I'm wondering if we can help you find some other ways of coping with your distress? (Criterion 3)
Example Response to Advanced Client Statement 2
Relapsing brings up such intense feelings of disappointment. (Criterion 1) Those feelings are so overwhelming that your brain escapes to thoughts of suicide. (Criterion 2) We've got to help you find a way to get your mind out of those unhelpful thoughts and manage those feelings of disappointment. (Criterion 3)
Example Response to Advanced Client Statement 3
You're feeling so ashamed. (Criterion 1) Those feelings make you just want to hide and kill yourself so you won't be seen and exposed. (Criterion 2) Can we look at this painful place of shame and disgust and figure out what this is about and how to help you address what's really going on? (Criterion 3)
Example Response to Advanced Client Statement 4
You're feeling out of control and afraid. (Criterion 1) The thought of suicide provides you with a sense of control and helps you feel less afraid. (Criterion 2) Can we look at what you can do right now to help you cope with those feelings of fear and powerlessness? (Criterion 3)
Example Response to Advanced Client Statement 5
I can hear that you're feeling so alone and it's painful. (Criterion 1) It's hard to tolerate those feelings; your mind tries to cope by focusing on thoughts of suicide and ending the pain. (Criterion 2) Can we help you figure out what you need to do to manage your loneliness without escaping it? (Criterion 3)

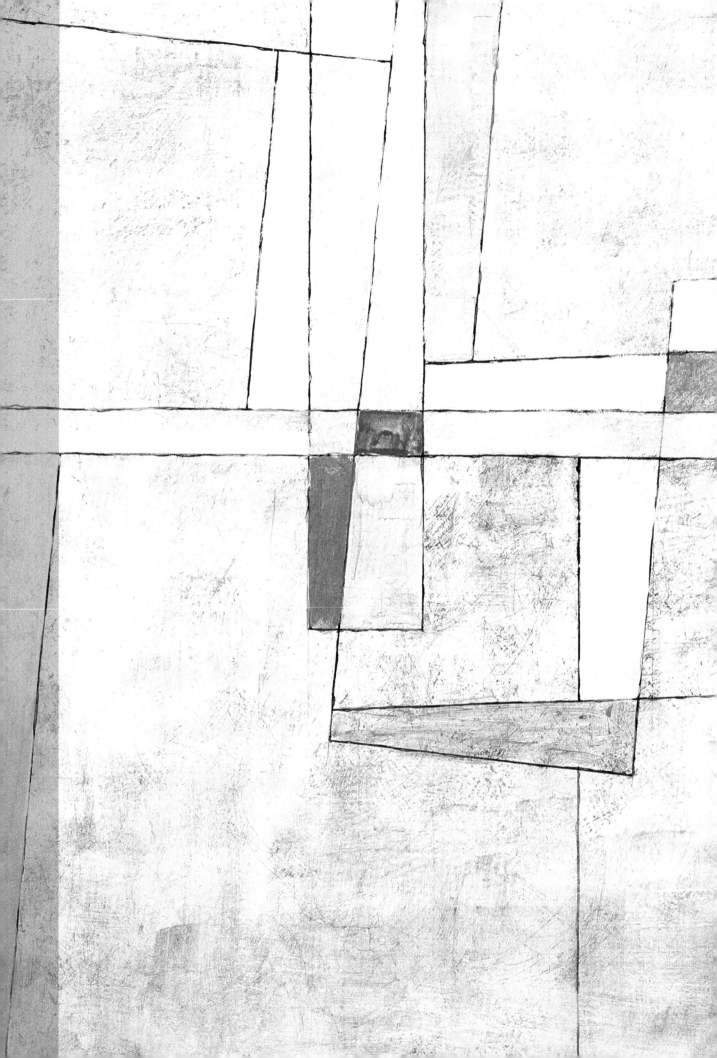

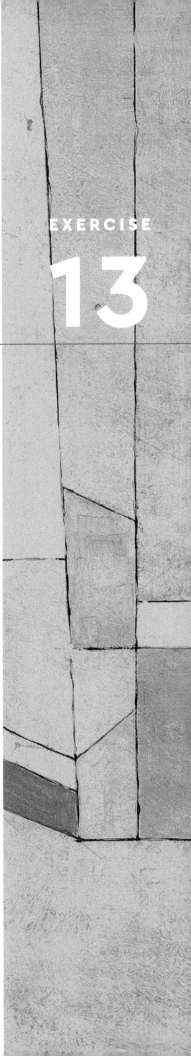

Annotated Dialectical Behavior Therapy Practice Session Transcript

It is now time to put together all the skills you have learned! This exercise presents a transcript from a dialectical behavior therapy (DBT) session. Each therapist statement is annotated to indicate which DBT skill from Exercises 1 through 12 is used. This transcript provides an example of how therapists can interweave many different DBT skills in response to clients.

Instructions

As in the previous exercises, one trainee plays the client, while the other plays the therapist. As much as possible, the trainee who plays the client should try to adopt an authentic emotional tone as if they were a real client. The first time through, both partners can read verbatim from the transcript. After one complete run-through, try it again. This time, the client can read from the script while the therapist can improvise to the degree that they feel comfortable. At this point, you may also want to reflect upon it with a supervisor and go through it again. Before you start, it is recommended that both the therapist and the client read the entire transcript through on your own, until the end. The purpose of the sample transcript is to give trainees the opportunity to try out what it is like to offer the DBT responses in a sequence that mimics live therapy sessions.

Note to Therapists

Remember to be aware of your vocal quality. Match your tone to the client's presentation. Thus, if the clients present vulnerable, soft emotions behind their words, soften your tone to be soothing and calm. If clients on the other hand, are aggressive and angry, match your tone to be firm.

https://doi.org/10.1037/0000322-015
Deliberate Practice in Dialectical Behavior Therapy, by T. Boritz, S. McMain, A. Vaz, and T. Rousmaniere

Annotated DBT Transcript

THERAPIST 1: Nice to see you today. Do you have your diary card?

CLIENT 1: [*pulls out diary card from bag and passes it to therapist*]

THERAPIST 2: Thank you. [*reading over diary card*] It looks like suicide urges were really high this week, yeah? OK and there was self-harm on most days but not all days. It looks like after our session you had really high urges to use, to quit, and to self-harm. That seems like something important for us to talk about. What do you think? What would you like to talk about today? What's on your agenda? (Skill 1: Establishing a Session Agenda)

CLIENT 2: [*looks nervous, feet are pointing inward, and hands are together at the center*] In group they were talking about the STOP skill, and I just find like there's no way for me to pause when I'm feeling messed up. Something just triggers me too fast and I'm not sure how to slow it down to be able to use something like that.

THERAPIST 3: OK, so it sounds like learning about that skill got you thinking about what happens in situations for you, and you're feeling like it's so automatic that it's hard to actually imagine introducing a pocket of time where you could do something differently. (Skill 2: Validation)

CLIENT 3: Yeah, exactly.

THERAPIST 4: OK, so let's definitely focus on that because you're right—it's really hard. It is hard to slow things down when it feels like something just happens automatically. (Skill 2: Validation) Even though it may feel automatic, sometimes there's a way to slow things down just enough. I have some ideas about how to do that, so perhaps we can put that on the agenda. If we have time, I'd also like to talk about what's been happening in our sessions that leaves you feeling more vulnerable afterward and sets off those high urges. Does that sound OK to you? (Skill 1: Establishing a Session Agenda)

CLIENT 4: [*whisper*] OK.

THERAPIST 5: So, where do you want to begin? What would be the most helpful place for you to begin? (Skill 1: Establishing a Session Agenda)

CLIENT 5: I'm not sure, to be honest.

THERAPIST 6: Maybe we can start by talking about the self-harm from last week and how to slow things down when you're feeling those really high urges to self-harm? (Skill 1: Establishing a Session Agenda)

CLIENT 6: [*slight nod*]

THERAPIST 7: OK, so it looks like you self-harmed on Tuesday and Wednesday, so is that yesterday or Tuesday and Wednesday of last week? (Skill 4: Problem Assessment, Criterion 2)

CLIENT 7: Last week.

THERAPIST 8: OK, is there one incident that happened this week that you think would be a good example for us to focus on? (Skill 4: Problem Assessment, Criterion 2)

CLIENT 8: [*pausing, hands together, playing with fingers*] Um, with my friend. We were at her house, she said something, and I got really upset and I just like . . . I don't know, it happens a lot where someone will say something and I would just freak out. And I would just go straight to like "I hate them," and then I am thinking about suicide after something that wasn't even a big deal, but it just happens so fast that I don't even understand.

THERAPIST 9: OK, so you were at your friend's house and something happened that made you feel really upset and led to thoughts of suicide. (Skill 2: Validation, Criterion 1) Can you tell me a bit more about what happened with your friend? Did she say something or do something that upset you? (Skill 4: Problem Assessment)

CLIENT 9: Um, she had to go out to do something and when she came back, I hadn't cleared the dishes from the table and she got upset that I should've done that.

THERAPIST 10: OK. Did she say something to you? (Skill 4: Problem Assessment, Criterion 2)

CLIENT 10: She told me she was disappointed.

THERAPIST 11: OK, so your friend said she was disappointed. Did she say anything else? (Skill 4: Problem Assessment, Criterion 2)

CLIENT 11: No.

THERAPIST 12: How did she say it? Was she yelling? Was her voice raised? (Skill 4: Problem Assessment, Criterion 2)

CLIENT 12: No.

THERAPIST 13: So she said she was disappointed with you? Or she said you hadn't cleared the table? (Skill 4: Problem Assessment, Criterion 2)

CLIENT 13: That I didn't clean the table.

THERAPIST 14: OK. And then what happened? (Skill 4: Problem Assessment, Criterion 2)

CLIENT 14: I was just like, I was just so angry, I was like . . .

THERAPIST 15: Angry? Was that the emotion you were feeling most strongly in that moment? (Skill 4: Problem Assessment, Criterion 2)

CLIENT 15: Yes.

THERAPIST 16: What was the anger about? (Skill 4: Problem Assessment, Criterion 2)

CLIENT 16: I didn't think it was fair that she was upset.

THERAPIST 17: What did you think was unfair about it? What was unfair about her being upset about you not clearing the table? (Skill 4: Problem Assessment, Criterion 2)

CLIENT 17: Because it wasn't like something I was supposed to do. It was something I could've done but I didn't really notice, and she obviously thought I didn't do it because I was lazy.

THERAPIST 18: So it sounds like you felt like you were being judged. (Skill 2: Validation, Criterion 1) Were there other emotions involved, other than anger? (Skill 4: Problem Assessment)

CLIENT 18: I don't know . . . I felt hurt.

THERAPIST 19: OK, what was the hurt about? Do you have a sense? What did you feel hurt about? (Skill 4: Problem Assessment, Criterion 2)

CLIENT 19: Because she was upset with me.

THERAPIST 20: And how did that make you feel hurt? (Skill 4: Problem Assessment, Criterion 2)

CLIENT 20: Because I don't like it when other people are upset with me.

THERAPIST 21: Yeah, that makes sense. I think it's hard. I mean I don't like it when other people are upset with me either. (Skill 2: Validation) But can you say more about the hurt? Like, "When I think of hurt, I think of sadness." (Skill 4: Problem Assessment, Criterion 1) Does that fit for you?

CLIENT 21: Um, just, it goes really fast and I am just like "I hate you." I just want to break stuff.

THERAPIST 22: OK, so there were urges to break stuff and to tell her you hated her. (Skill 2: Validation, Criterion 1) Did you actually tell her that you hated her? (Skill 4: Problem Assessment)

CLIENT 22: No, at that point I was by myself, it was just like anger and thinking I hate her.

THERAPIST 23: OK. So, it sounds like, if I'm understanding it correctly, your friend came home and was upset that you hadn't cleared the table, which then upset you because that wasn't something you thought was your responsibility to do. (Skill 2: Validation) It wasn't something you were aware of or thought about doing, and that prompted distress. Is that correct? Am I understanding that correctly? (Skill 4: Problem Assessment, Criterion 1)

CLIENT 23: Yeah, maybe because I didn't go in the kitchen while she was out, so I didn't even really notice the dishes.

THERAPIST 24: OK, and it sounds like you were thinking she was disappointed that you didn't clear the table and that left you feeling hurt and angry. It sounds like you were feeling angry because it didn't feel fair that she was upset with you because you didn't really think you had done anything wrong, and this led to urges to break stuff and lash out. (Skill 2: Validation; Skill 8: Modifying Cognitions, Criteria 1 and 2) What happened after that? What happened after you felt those urges? Did you express any of those feelings to your friend? (Skill 4: Problem Assessment)

CLIENT 24: [*pause*] I didn't go and tell her that I was angry, but she could see that I was.

THERAPIST 25: How could she see you were angry? What was she noticing? (Skill 4: Problem Assessment, Criterion 2)

CLIENT 25: [*pause*] 'Cause I was throwing things.

THERAPIST 26: Ah, that's too bad. You had the urge to break stuff and then you did it, you did break some stuff. What were you throwing? (Skill 2: Validation, Criterion 1; Skill 4: Problem Assessment)

CLIENT 26: I don't think I broke anything.

THERAPIST 27: Oh, sorry, I misunderstood. So what were you throwing? (Skill 4: Problem Assessment, Criterion 2)

CLIENT 27: I don't know, just stuff around the room . . . I was just angry.

THERAPIST 28: Ah, OK, so you were feeling angry and started throwing stuff around the room. (Skill 2: Validation, Criterion 1) Were there other anger behaviors that you were doing? Yelling, or swearing, or doing anything like that? (Skill 4: Problem Assessment)

CLIENT 28: [*pause*] Um, I don't remember. But someone said I pushed her.

THERAPIST 29: You pushed her? (Skill 4: Problem Assessment, Criterion 2)

CLIENT 29: I don't remember specifically.

THERAPIST 30: And then what happened? (Skill 4: Problem Assessment, Criterion 2)

CLIENT 30: I was just like, fuming, I hated her so much and then I was—I just wanted to die.

THERAPIST 31: Then what happened? (Skill 4: Problem Assessment, Criterion 2)

CLIENT 31: And then I burned myself.

THERAPIST 32: So when did that happen? Was that after you were throwing stuff or was that in between? (Skill 4: Problem Assessment, Criterion 2)

CLIENT 32: It was after.

THERAPIST 33: OK, so you were feeling so angry and had thoughts of wanting to die. (Skill 2: Validation, Criterion 1) How did you get to burning yourself? What was the link there? You were having thoughts "I hate her so much" and "I want to die" and . . . and then how did you get to burning yourself? (Skill 4: Problem Assessment; Skill 8: Modifying Cognitions, Criteria 1 and 2)

CLIENT 33: Because I was thinking this really hurts.

THERAPIST 34: OK, so your distress went up, your pain went up. (Skill 2: Validation, Criterion 1) And how did you get to burning yourself as a solution? What was the connection—how did you decide to do that? (Skill 4: Problem Assessment)

CLIENT 34: 'Cause I can't handle thinking like that.

THERAPIST 35: OK, so that was part of it, the thought "I can't handle these thoughts." (Skill 2: Validation) Were there any other thoughts you are aware of? (Skill 4: Problem Assessment; Skill 8: Modifying Cognitions, Criterion 1)

CLIENT 35: Just like, "Everybody hates me—why am I here trying?"

THERAPIST 36: And then what happened? Where did you hurt yourself? (Skill 4: Problem Assessment, Criterion 2)

CLIENT 36: Um, my arms.

THERAPIST 37: With a lighter? (Skill 4: Problem Assessment, Criterion 2)

CLIENT 37: [*slight nod*]

THERAPIST 38: And then what happened? (Skill 4: Problem Assessment, Criterion 2)

CLIENT 38: I was still angry.

THERAPIST 39: You were still angry at your friend. (Skill 2: Validation, Criterion 1) Were you less angry? (Skill 4: Problem Assessment, Criterion 2)

CLIENT 39: Yeah.

THERAPIST 40: What else, what else happened?

CLIENT 40: It really hurt. Then I saw her, and she wasn't angry at me anymore. She asked me something and wasn't angry at me anymore.

THERAPIST 41: Were you still angry at her? (Skill 4: Problem Assessment, Criterion 2)

CLIENT 41: [*nods*]

THERAPIST 42: You were still angry. (Skill 2: Validation, Criterion 1) What were you still angry about? (Skill 4: Problem Assessment, Criterion 2)

CLIENT 42: Because she got angry at me.

THERAPIST 43: And did you tell her that, or did you keep it in? (Skill 4: Problem Assessment, Criterion 2)

CLIENT 43: I didn't tell her. She had to leave.

THERAPIST 44: When we started today's session, one of your questions was how do you find a way to introduce some kind of pause so that you can stop the urges—or not stop the urges necessarily, but stop the actions that go with the urges. It sounds like it can feel like a big blur once the process gets started, it's like your emotions are a runaway train a bit. (Skill 2: Validation, Criterion 1; Skill 6: Problem Solving, Criterion 1) No wonder it feels in the moment like it's all happening automatically. (Skill 2: Validation)

CLIENT 44: Yeah.

THERAPIST 45: OK, so listening to all this, I have a couple of ideas about how to do that. But one thought I'm having . . . I'm wondering a bit about hurt and sadness, and if those were the feelings that were causing you pain, even though the anger was the one that you felt more strongly. It was really painful to have your friend be upset with you. (Skill 2: Validation) But I'm also wondering if there was another emotion in the mix. Was there shame that got activated? (Skill 4: Problem Assessment)

CLIENT 45: [*nods*]

THERAPIST 46: OK. So it's almost like when you feel ashamed, it's so hard to feel it. Almost unbearable. (Skill 2: Validation, Criterion 1) Maybe anger feels a little bit easier than shame to manage in some ways. (Skill 6: Problem Solving, Criterion 1) I don't know . . . does that sound like it fits? [*pause*]

CLIENT 46: Yeah.

THERAPIST 47: OK, so it was almost like the first things you felt were shame and sadness and then anger kind of took over, which felt a little bit better than feeling such intense shame. (Skill 2: Validation, Criterion 1) I wonder if instead of having to sit with that feeling that your friend was upset with you—or that maybe you had done something wrong—it was easier in a way to get angry at your friend for making you feel that way. (Skill 6: Problem Solving, Criterion 1) I don't know, does that fit for you? What are your thoughts about that?

CLIENT 47: [*pause*] Yeah, I think that happens a lot. And I get confused because I'm not sure if she's right or I'm right.

THERAPIST 48: Right, because the shame gets set off and it's so painful and there's this part of you that's like, "Wait a minute—I didn't do anything wrong, I don't deserve this feeling." It makes sense that you might feel angry if you're having the thought "How dare you make me feel this way, I feel so bad right now and I didn't even do anything wrong." (Skill 2: Validation)

CLIENT 48: Yeah, like blaming her for making me feel bad.

THERAPIST 49: So, what's kind of cool about us being able to identify this. [*pause*] (Skill 3: Reinforcing Adaptive Behavior) Hmm . . . I'm looking at you and noticing you've sort of sunken into your chair and I can't see your face anymore. (Skill 2: Validation, Criterion 1) I'm guessing it's hard to talk about this stuff with me? I am wondering if the shame is activated right here right now. Is it happening right now? (Skill 9: Informal Exposure to Emotion, Criterion 1)

CLIENT 49: [*makes eye contact, nods slightly*]

THERAPIST 50: OK, I am so glad that you just made eye contact with me because that was the perfect way of acting the opposite to shame. (Skill 3: Reinforcing Adaptive Behavior) How intense is the shame right now? On a scale from 1 to 10? (Skill 9: Informal Exposure to Emotion, Criterion 1)

CLIENT 50: It's high, like an 8.

THERAPIST 51: OK, the shame is really high right now. (Skill 2: Validation, Criterion 1) Why don't you try taking a few deep breaths to see if that helps bring the emotion down a bit? (Skill 10: Coaching Clients in Distress—Criterion 2, Paced Breathing skill)

CLIENT 51: [*client spends a few seconds breathing*]

THERAPIST 52: Is that helping?

CLIENT 52: Yeah, a bit.

THERAPIST 53: OK, so it makes sense that shame got activated because we started talking about something that made you feel vulnerable (Skill 2: Validation) and, I don't know, maybe embarrassed? (Skill 4: Problem Assessment, Criterion 2) Is there anything else you can do right now to just connect to that painful feeling without escaping it? (Skill 9: Informal Exposure to Emotion; Skill 6: Inviting the Client to Engage in Problem Solving) If the feeling is getting too intense, you can try picking up that ice pack and holding it to your temple (Skill 10: Coaching Clients in Distress—Criterion 2, Temperature skill)

CLIENT 53: [*slight nod; picks up ice pack and applies it to their temple*]

THERAPIST 54: OK, so what I would like you to do is, when you're noticing that shame feeling coming up, try to just notice it, without judging it or trying to change it. (Skill 7: Skills Training—Mindfulness) Shame is a feeling that says, "I have done something wrong, and I am bad." For a lot of people, it's a feeling that's learned—not actually related to what you did. It makes sense that that feeling might come up if you're having thoughts like that. (Skill 2: Validation) Is anything like that happening for you right now?

CLIENT 54: [*pause*] Maybe.

THERAPIST 55: Maybe. What do you think you have done wrong? (Skill 4: Problem Assessment, Criterion 2)

CLIENT 55: I'm thinking maybe you think I did something wrong too. Maybe you think that I should've put the dishes away too.

THERAPIST 56: Ah, so you're having the worry thought that maybe I'm judging you as well and thinking that you should've done something differently. (Skill 2: Validation, Criterion 1; Skill 8: Modifying Cognitions, Criterion 1) That's a painful thought to have. If I thought my therapist was judging me, I'd probably be feeling a lot of shame too. (Skill 2: Validation; Skill 8: Modifying Cognitions, Criteria 1 and 2)

CLIENT 56: Yeah.

THERAPIST 57: I'm wondering . . . do you want to check in with me about that? Do you want to check that out with me directly? To see if I am actually thinking that? (Skill 6: Problem Solving, Criterion 2; Skill 8: Modifying Cognitions, Criterion 3)

CLIENT 57: Not really.

THERAPIST 58: No, OK. It sounds like it feels too much right now. (Skill 2: Validation, Criterion 1) Is the shame going up even at the thought of having to say that? (Skill 4: Problem Assessment, Criterion 2)

CLIENT 58: [slight nod]

THERAPIST 59: OK, so what can you do to bring yourself back into the present moment with me—to notice those worry thoughts and to try to interrupt them? (Skill 8: Modifying Cognitions, Criterion 3) Do you want to check in with me visually? (Skill 6: Problem Solving, Criterion 2) I'm wondering if looking at me might help. Because right now your eyes are down, and it's probably helping bring that shame down a bit and easier to stay stuck in those worry thoughts. (Skill 11: Promoting Dialectical Thinking Through Both–And Statements) If you can, can you look at me? Shame might get more intense, and if you can try to stay with the feeling without escaping or avoiding it. (Skill 9: Informal Exposure to Emotion)

CLIENT 59: [looks at therapist]

THERAPIST 60: Good—you're doing great. (Skill 3: Reinforcing Adaptive Behavior) Now, if you can, can you try to describe what you see? What is my face doing? What does my voice sound like? What words am I saying?

CLIENT 60: [keeps looking at therapist, silently]

THERAPIST 61: That's great. Keep those eyes on me if you can. (Skill 9: Informal Exposure to Emotion) Do I look like I am angry or disappointed? Do I look upset at you? Do I sound upset at you?

CLIENT 61: No.

THERAPIST 62: OK, well that's important information to pay attention to. Sometimes we can have thoughts or really strong feelings about what's happening that are different from what actually is happening. Does that make sense? That you can feel an emotion really strongly, and it might be valid—like it might make sense given the thoughts you're having, or given past experiences—but it might not totally fit what's actually happening in the moment? (Skill 8: Modifying Cognitions)

CLIENT 62: Yes.

THERAPIST 63: Given some of the things you've told me about how you grew up, it sounds like there were a lot of times you got told you were doing something wrong, or when people got angry at you for no reason, and it makes perfect sense to me that that fear comes up now. With other people, but also with me—that at any moment I'm going to turn around and blame you for something. (Skill 2: Validation) Does that make sense to you? That it's like perfectly natural to have that fear or concern if that was the message you got growing up. (Skill 2: Validation)

CLIENT 63: [slight head nod]

THERAPIST 64: So even here in our sessions, it sounds like it sort of comes up automatically before you've even had the chance to notice the emotion or think it through. (Skill 4: Problem Assessment, Criterion 2) What are you feeling right now as we are talking? (Skill 9: Informal Exposure to Emotion, Criterion 1)

CLIENT 64: [Pause] It's kind of hard.

THERAPIST 65: Yeah, what's hard?

CLIENT 65: Something I am doing makes things hard.

THERAPIST 66: Ah, OK. I think I understand that too. Does it sound like a criticism? Like I'm saying you're doing something wrong here by feeling that way? (Skill 4: Problem Assessment, Criterion 2)

CLIENT 66: Kind of. I don't know.

THERAPIST 67: OK, so I think maybe that's the shame getting activated again. (Skill 9: Informal Exposure to Emotion, Criterion 1) Like maybe it's feeling like I'm saying you should be doing something differently?

CLIENT 67: Yeah, like I'm not supposed to think that way. Like there's something wrong with me. When I start feeling that way, I just want to die. It's like, what's the point? I'm so broken.

THERAPIST 68: Mmm . . . yeah that feeling is so intense, almost unbearable. It sounds like thinking about being dead brings some relief to that painful feeling. No wonder your mind goes there. (Skill 2: Validation) I'd like to work with you to find a better way to find relief from your pain. Is that something you would want? (Skill 12: Responding to Suicidal Ideation; Skill 5: Eliciting a Commitment)

CLIENT 68: Yes. I don't want to feel this way all the time.

THERAPIST 69: I'm really glad to hear you say that. (Skill 3: Reinforcing Adaptive Behavior) You know, it's interesting. It sounds like what set off those thoughts were feelings of shame that I was judging you. (Skill 8: Modifying Cognitions, Criteria 1 and 2) I was actually having a completely different thought. What I am thinking right now is that it's pretty fantastic you've been able to identify those thoughts and feelings and talk to me about them even though it's been hard, because now we can actually work on this stuff together. (Skill 3: Reinforcing Adaptive Behavior)

CLIENT 69: I guess so.

THERAPIST 70: I'm wondering if this is something you would be willing to work on with me? Trying to notice what you're thinking or feeling without judging or criticizing it? Is that something you would be willing to practice? (Skill 5: Eliciting a Commitment; Skill 6: Problem Solving)

CLIENT 70: I can try.

THERAPIST 71: That's great. (Skill 3: Reinforcing Adaptive Behavior) Something we can also continue working on down the road is getting you to not just notice when an emotion like shame comes up, but to then ask yourself if it's related to something that's happening here and now, or if it's an old response, an automatic response, which makes sense given your history but either doesn't fit or it's too intense for the present situation.

CLIENT 71: I think that will be hard to do.

THERAPIST 72: Yes, I'm sure it will be hard at first. It's not easy to catch these automatic responses. And I saw you begin to do it today, so I feel really confident that if you keep working at it, it'll get easier to do. (Skill 3: Reinforcing Adaptive Behavior)

CLIENT 72: OK.

THERAPIST 73: So, I'm wondering if we can turn our focus back to self-harm. You said that after that fight with your friend you burned yourself. We kind of worked through how your emotions got so intense and led to urges to self-harm. You also mentioned that you had the thought "I can't handle this," which makes sense and maybe tipped you over the edge. (Skill 2: Validation; Skill 4: Problem Assessment, Criterion 1)

CLIENT 73: [nods]

THERAPIST 74: One thing I was wondering about was ways to decrease the likelihood of self-harm when you're feeling so intense and having strong urges. Last week, the self-harm—was it just burning, or was there cutting too? (Skill 4: Problem Assessment, Criterion 2)

CLIENT 74: No, just burning.

THERAPIST 75: OK, and always with a lighter? Or with other things too? (Skill 4: Problem Assessment, Criterion 2)

CLIENT 75: Just with the lighter. And like, I don't need it around. I don't smoke.

THERAPIST 76: I'm so glad to hear you say that. (Skill 3: Reinforcing Adaptive Behavior) I was thinking the same thing! It sounds like those lighters don't need to be around the house. When they're there, it's like a cue for self-harm thoughts. Can we get rid of them? (Skill 6: Problem Solving)

CLIENT 76: I mean, I don't smoke, but we use them for the BBQ.

THERAPIST 77: OK, it sounds like you're saying you're not sure if you can get rid of them? (Skill 4: Problem Assessment, Criterion 2)

CLIENT 77: [silent]

THERAPIST 78: OK, let me take a step back to see if I understand. If we could figure out the BBQ thing, is getting rid of the lighters or any of the things you use to self-harm some-thing you would be willing to do? To help buy you time to use skills when your urges are really high? (Skill 5: Eliciting a Commitment; Skill 6: Problem Solving)

CLIENT 78: I don't know. Maybe.

THERAPIST 79: OK, I can work with that. [smiles] One thought is that if you're not ready to get rid of them completely, you could put them in a place that's hard to get to. Where in your house would lighters be hard to get to? (Skill 6: Problem Solving)

CLIENT 79: I guess the basement. I don't like to go down there. It's full of bugs and creeps me out.

THERAPIST 80: That's a great idea! (Skill 3: Reinforcing Adaptive Behavior) Could you put them in a box and move them to the basement? (Skill 6: Problem Solving, Criterion 2)

CLIENT 80: Yeah, I could do that.

THERAPIST 81: Amazing. (Skill 3: Reinforcing Adaptive Behavior) If you wanted to go a step further, you could put even more obstacles to getting them. Like locking them in a box in the basement or wrapping them up in a bag with tape so they're not so easy to get out. Could you do that? (Skill 6: Problem Solving, Criterion 2)

CLIENT 81: I think I can do that.

THERAPIST 82: Yeah? Fantastic. (Skill 3: Reinforcing Adaptive Behavior) What could get in the way of you actually doing that when you leave here today? (Skill 4: Problem Assessment, Criterion 2)

CLIENT 82: I don't know. I can do it with my lighters, but what about the other lighters in my house? My roommates have them everywhere.

THERAPIST 83: Ah, this is a great question! (Skill 3: Reinforcing Adaptive Behavior) Are your roommates people you could talk to about what you're doing and why you're doing it? Are they people that could support you around doing it? (Skill 4: Problem Assessment, Criterion 2)

CLIENT 83: [*pause*] They don't know I use the lighter.

THERAPIST 84: They don't know? Do they know that you self-harm? (Skill 4: Problem Assessment, Criterion 2)

CLIENT 84: [*nod*]

THERAPIST 85: OK, so it sounds like if you told them you self-harm with lighters maybe it wouldn't be such a surprise? (Skill 4: Problem Assessment, Criterion 2)

CLIENT 85: It's so embarrassing.

THERAPIST 86: Yeah, I can imagine it wouldn't be the most comfortable conversation and it might be worth doing it anyway. (Skill 11: Promoting Dialectical Thinking Through Both–And Statements) I mean in some ways it ties in really nicely with what we've been talking about today. Acting opposite to shame . . . and maybe showing yourself that you can do hard things even if it brings up change.

CLIENT 86: I guess so. I'll think about it.

THERAPIST 87: OK, it sounds like you're committed to getting rid of your lighters but are a bit less sure about talking to your roommates about getting rid of their lighters. I can understand that. (Skill 2: Validation) I think it's really great that you're willing to get rid of yours, (Skill 3: Reinforcing Adaptive Behavior) and perhaps next week we can focus a bit more on how to get rid of the ones that don't belong to you or that your roommates bring into the house. So it sounds like between now and next week you'll put your lighters in the basement and will consider talking to your roommates. Is that correct?

CLIENT 87: Yes, I will do that.

THERAPIST 88: Great! If it would be helpful, you can email me after you've done it to let me know. Do you think that would increase the likelihood of you doing it? (Skill 3: Reinforcing Adaptive Behavior)

CLIENT 88: I think so.

THERAPIST 89: OK, fantastic. I'll look forward to getting that email. (Skill 3: Reinforcing Adaptive Behavior) So I think the last thing we should focus on before we wrap up today is this thought: "I can't handle these thoughts." It sounds like when that thought popped up last week it left you feeling kind of hopeless and like you had no option but to self-harm. (Skill 8: Modifying Cognitions) Can you remind me, have you learned distress tolerance skills in your group yet?

CLIENT 89: [*head shake*]

THERAPIST 90: No? OK, these might be the perfect skills to use when you have the thought "I can't handle this." Because one of the things we're doing when we use distress tolerance skills is saying "my emotions are really intense right now, but feelings pass, they're like waves." So maybe in those moments where you notice the thought "I can't handle this," you can try to validate yourself by acknowledging "this is so hard" or "this is such a painful feeling, and it's hard to feel." I wonder if that would help you feel more motivated in the moment to try to use a skill. Like grabbing an ice pack or taking a cold shower. Have you tried doing either of those things when you're feeling distressed? (Skill 6: Problem Solving; Skill 7: Skills Training; Skill 10: Coaching Clients in Distress—Criterion 2, Temperature skill)

CLIENT 90: Yeah, I tried that a bit last week.

THERAPIST 91: That's amazing! (Skill 3: Reinforcing Adaptive Behavior) Was it helpful?

CLIENT 91: I mean, I don't know. I still self-harmed.

THERAPIST 92: Uh huh. I see. So it didn't help interrupt the action. Did it buy you any time in between the urge and action? (Skill 4: Problem Assessment)

CLIENT 92: [*pause*] Yes.

THERAPIST 93: OK. That's a great start. (Skill 3: Reinforcing Adaptive Behavior) What we can talk about next time is other skills you can use in that brief period of time that might tip the balance. How does that sound to you?

CLIENT 93: That sounds good. It's just difficult.

THERAPIST 94: It is difficult. It is absolutely difficult. (Skill 2: Validation) The goal here is not to become an expert overnight. It's to keep practicing and seeing what works and then readjusting and adding new things if what you're doing isn't working or if it needs to be tweaked. This is hard stuff, and I know you can do it. (Skill 11: Promoting Dialectical Thinking Through Both–And Statements) And I'm here to help you do it. So we have a bunch of stuff that we need to revisit on the agenda next week 'cause I really do want to understand what's happening in our sessions that is increasing your urges to use, and to quit therapy and self-harm. Are you having those high urges right now? (Skill 4: Problem Assessment, Criterion 2)

CLIENT 94: [*pause*] It's hard.

THERAPIST 95: Yeah? Are you having those high urges right now though?

CLIENT 95: It's like, I've never had a chance to understand how to grow, but it's scary at the same time.

THERAPIST 96: Yeah, that makes total sense to me. It's scary to try to do new things, especially when you don't know what to expect or are worried it's not going to work for you. (Skill 2: Validation) And I think it's amazing that you keep coming and trying despite how scared you feel. Just showing up sometimes takes a lot of effort and courage. (Skill 3: Reinforcing Adaptive Behavior)

CLIENT 96: Yeah.

THERAPIST 97: So, there's a lot on your plate this week. You're going to get rid of or put the lighters away and let me know once you've done that. Are there any other pieces from today that you are thinking would be helpful to focus on this coming week? Perhaps one other thing that we talked about that you think you'd like to focus on? (Skill 6: Problem Solving, Criterion 2)

CLIENT 97: [*pause*] Maybe tracking when I am feeling embarrassed.

THERAPIST 98: I think that's a great idea. (Skill 3: Reinforcing Adaptive Behavior) Keeping track of embarrassment and shame and perhaps noticing urges that go along with that feeling?

CLIENT 98: Yeah.

THERAPIST 99: Well, I am really looking forward to hearing how that goes and what you notice. You and I are meeting at our regular time next week, yeah? Here's a new diary card.

CLIENT 99: OK. Thank you.

THERAPIST 100: You're welcome; I'll see you next week.

CLIENT 100: See you next week.

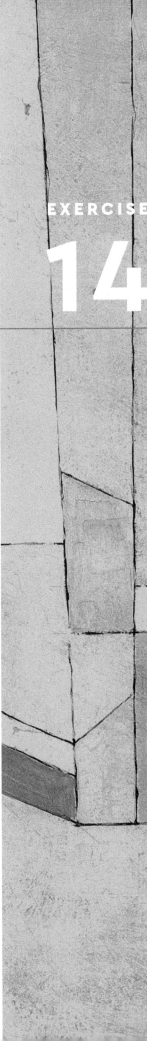

Mock Dialectical Behavior Therapy Sessions

In contrast to highly structured and repetitive deliberate practice exercises, a mock dialectical behavior therapy (DBT) session is an unstructured and improvised role-play therapy session. Like a jazz rehearsal, mock sessions let you practice the art and science of *appropriate responsiveness* (Hatcher, 2015; Stiles & Horvath, 2017), putting your psychotherapy skills together in a way that is helpful to your mock client. This exercise outlines the procedure for conducting a mock DBT session. It offers different client profiles you may choose to adopt when role-playing a client.

Mock sessions are an opportunity for trainees to practice the following:

- using psychotherapy skills responsively
- navigating challenging choice points in therapy
- choosing which interventions to use
- tracking the arc of a therapy session and the overall big-picture therapy treatment
- guiding treatment in the context of the client's preferences
- determining realistic goals for therapy in the context of the client's capacities
- knowing how to proceed when the therapist is unsure, lost, or confused
- recognizing and recovering from therapeutic errors
- discovering your personal therapeutic style
- building endurance for working with real clients

Mock DBT Session Overview

For the mock session, **you will perform a role-play of an initial therapy session.** As is true with the exercises to build individual skills, the role-play involves three people: One trainee role-plays the therapist, another trainee role-plays the client, and a trainer (a professor or a supervisor) observes and provides feedback. This is an open-ended role-play, as is commonly done in training. However, it differs in two important ways from the role-plays used in more traditional training. First, the therapist will use their

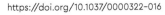

https://doi.org/10.1037/0000322–016

Deliberate Practice in Dialectical Behavior Therapy, by T. Boritz, S. McMain, A. Vaz, and T. Rousmaniere

hand to indicate how difficult the role-play feels. Second, the client will attempt to make the role-play easier or harder to ensure the therapist is practicing at the right difficulty level.

Preparation

1. Read the instructions in Chapter 2.

2. Download the Deliberate Practice Reaction Form and the Deliberate Practice Diary Form from the "Clinician and Practitioner Resources" tab at https://www.apa.org/pubs/books/deliberate-practice-dialectical-behavior-therapy (also available in Appendixes A and B, respectively). Every student will need their own copy of the Deliberate Practice Reaction Form on a separate piece of paper so they can access it quickly.

3. Designate one student to role-play the therapist and one student to role-play the client. The trainer will observe and provide corrective feedback.

Mock DBT Session Procedure

1. The trainees will role-play an initial (first) therapy session. The trainee role-playing the client selects a client profile from the end of this exercise.

2. Before beginning the role-play, the therapist raises their hand to their side, at the level of their chair seat (see Figure E14.1). They will use this hand throughout the role-play to indicate how challenging it feels to them to help the client. Their starting hand level

FIGURE E14.1. Ongoing Difficulty Assessment Through Hand Level

Note. Left: Start of role-play. Right: Role-play is too difficult. Reprinted from *Deliberate Practice in Emotion-Focused Therapy* (p. 156), by R. N. Goldman, A. Vaz, and T. Rousmaniere, 2021, American Psychological Association (https://doi.org/10.1037/0000227–000). Copyright 2021 by the American Psychological Association.

(chair seat) indicates that the role-play feels easy. By raising their hand, the therapist indicates that the difficulty is rising. If their hand rises above their neck level, it indicates that the role-play is too difficult.

3. The therapist begins the role-play. The therapist and client should engage in the role-play in an improvised manner, as they would engage in a real therapy session. The therapist keeps their hand out at their side throughout this process. (This may feel strange at first!)

4. Whenever the therapist feels that the difficulty of the role-play has changed significantly, they should move their hand up if it feels more difficult and down if it feels easier. If the therapist's hand drops below the seat of their chair, the client should make the role-play more challenging; if the therapist's hand rises above their neck level, the client should make the role-play easier. Instructions for adjusting the difficulty of the role-play are described in the Varying the Level of Challenge section.

Note to Therapists

Remember to be aware of your vocal tone and pacing. Match your tone to the client's presentation. Thus, if clients present softer emotions, soften your tone to be soothing and calm. If, on the other hand, clients are demonstrating more volatility, match your tone to be firm and solid. If you choose responses that prompt client exploration, remember to adopt a more querying, exploratory tone of voice.

---

5. The role-play continues for at least 15 minutes. The trainer may provide corrective feedback during this process if the therapist gets significantly offtrack. However, trainers should exercise restraint and keep feedback as short and tight as possible, as this will increase the therapist's opportunity for experiential training.

6. After the role-play is finished, the therapist and client switch roles and begin a new mock session.

7. After both trainees have completed the mock session as a therapist, the trainees and the trainer discuss the experience.

Varying the Level of Challenge

If the therapist indicates that the mock session is too easy, the person enacting the role of the client can use the following modifications to make it more challenging (see also Appendix A):

*   The client can improvise with topics that are more evocative or make the therapist uncomfortable, such as expressing currently held strong feelings (see Figure A.2).
*   The client can use a distressed voice (e.g., angry, sad, sarcastic) or unpleasant facial expression. This increases the emotional tone.
*   The client can blend complex mixtures of opposing feelings (e.g., love and rage).
*   The client can become confrontational, questioning the purpose of therapy or the therapist's fitness for the role.

If the therapist indicates that the mock session is too hard:

- The client can be guided by Figure A.2 to
  - present topics that are less evocative,
  - present material on any topic but without expressing feelings, or
  - present material concerning the future or the past or events outside therapy.

- The client can ask the questions in a soft voice or with a smile. This softens the emotional stimulus.

- The therapist can take short breaks during the role-play.

- The trainer can expand the "feedback phase" by discussing DBT or psychotherapy theory.

Mock Session Client Profiles

Following are six client profiles for trainees to use during mock sessions, presented in order of difficulty. The choice of client profile may be determined by the trainee playing the therapist, the trainee playing the client, or assigned by the trainer.

The most important aspect of role-plays is for trainees to convey the emotional tone indicated by the client profile (e.g., "angry" or "sad"). The demographics of the client and specific content of the client profiles are not important. Thus, trainees should adjust the client profile to be most comfortable and easy for the trainee to role-play. For example, a trainee may change the gender, age, or cultural background included in the client profile.

Beginner Profile: Working With Sadness With a Receptive Client

Annie is a 28-year-old Asian woman who recently broke up with her boyfriend. She has been feeling sadness about the end of her relationship. Her sadness is complicated by feelings of anger that her boyfriend betrayed her by breaking up with her "out of the blue." She described feeling very attached to her boyfriend when they were together despite a lot of volatility in the relationship (e.g., frequent conflict and arguments). She feels rejected by her boyfriend and has tried many times to convince him to take her back, including multiple text messages and phone calls. So far, he has been unresponsive to her attempts to reconcile. Annie wants help coping more effectively with her sadness and anger.

- **Symptoms:** Sadness, anger, shame, and loneliness
- **Client's goals for therapy:** Annie wants to cope more effectively with her emotions related to her breakup.
- **Attitude toward therapy:** Annie has had good experiences in therapy in the past and is optimistic about therapy helping again.
- **Strengths:** Annie is motivated to work on her own problematic behaviors.

Beginner Profile: Working With an Anxious and Engaged Client

Firaz is a 25-year-old Middle Eastern man who experiences anxiety, occasional panic attacks, and high levels of shame. He says he has felt like a "loser" his whole life. He was bullied in high school and often feels like people are judging him. As a result, he tries to avoid contact with people except through online computer games. He lives at home with his parents, and they suggested that he come to therapy because they were concerned he was spending too much time by himself. Firaz says he would like more social connection but doesn't think other people would be interested in being friends with him.

- **Symptoms:** Anxiety and shame

- **Client's goals for therapy:** Firaz wants to decrease anxiety and increase social connections.

- **Attitude toward therapy:** Firaz has not received any previous treatment. He is uncertain what to expect from therapy. He feels anxious about attending therapy but is hopeful it will help.

- **Strengths:** Firaz is cautious but open-minded and motivated to engage in the therapy tasks.

Intermediate Profile: Working With a Shame-Prone and Ambivalent Client

Dani is a 30-year-old White, nonbinary individual who experiences extreme shame, anxiety, and depression. While growing up, they struggled to fit in with their peers in their small town and felt they had to hide their gender identity and sexual orientation from both family and friends. Since moving to an urban center, they are finally living their life in a way that feels authentic and in a community they feel accepts them. Nevertheless, they are sensitive to rejection and often respond with extreme reactions when they feel judged or invalidated by others. For example, they will end relationships or quit jobs impulsively then regret it afterward.

- **Symptoms:** Shame, anxiety, and depression

- **Client's goals for therapy:** Dani wants to feel more confident socially so they can engage in work and social relationships more reliably.

- **Attitude toward therapy:** Dani initially didn't want to come to therapy because they worried their therapist would judge them. A close friend of theirs convinced them to give therapy a try.

- **Strengths:** Underneath their shame and anxiety, Dani desires a connection with other people, including their therapist.

Intermediate Profile: Working With an Angry Client

Maria is a 55-year-old Latinx woman who was referred to DBT by her psychiatrist because previous treatments had been unsuccessful. Maria is very smart and gets frustrated quickly when people challenge her, patronize her, or when she feels misunderstood. When she gets frustrated, Maria can get sarcastic or mean. Not infrequently, she can become so enraged that she has anger outbursts that include name-calling, swearing, and physical aggression. Maria understands that this is a problem and would like to be more in control of her anger, but she has been unable to change her behavior. She also feels resentful that she is the one who needs to change her behavior because she believes her anger is often triggered by others' mistreatment of her.

- **Symptoms:** Anger, shame, sadness, and loneliness
- **Client's goals for therapy:** Maria wants to decrease her anger, improve her relationships with others, and feel less depressed.

- **Attitude toward therapy:** Maria has been in therapy before and is skeptical that this new treatment will help; however, she feels it's her last hope.
- **Strengths:** Maria is a smart and sensitive person and wants a better life for herself with less suffering.

Advanced Profile: Working With a Mistrustful and Withdrawn Client

Bea is a 27-year-old Black woman and the oldest of four siblings. Bea and her siblings were sexually and physically abused by her father when she was a child. Her father also beat her mother frequently, and this intensified once Bea left home. She does not generally trust the system because she has not felt her interests have been prioritized or protected. She experiences intense anxiety and panic when she leaves the house and often appears withdrawn and dissociative in her therapy sessions. She uses alcohol to manage overwhelming emotional states. She feels confused about her feelings toward her mother: She feels angry that her mother did not protect her from her father, and she feels guilty because she abandoned her mother when she left home.

- **Symptoms:** Anxiety, dissociation, shame, anger at parents, and guilt about abandoning her mother

- **Client's goals for therapy:** Bea wants to decrease anxiety and dissociation, process her traumas, and resolve her anger and guilt toward her mother.

- **Attitude toward therapy:** Bea saw a counselor while she was in high school but had a bad experience: When she told her counselor about her father's abuse, her counselor told her parents what she had said, and they denied it. Thus, Bea is very mistrustful of therapists.

- **Strengths:** Bea is committed to improving her mental health. She attends sessions regularly and completes homework reliably.

Advanced Profile: Working With a Client With Emotion Dysregulation and Self-Harm Behaviors

Jane is a 20-year-old White woman who is having problems in her friendships. She cycles between intense feelings of closeness with her friends and then hating them when they do something that upsets her or when she feels left out or unimportant, like when they make plans without her or cancel plans. When Jane feels rejected by her friends, she feels betrayed and abandoned, gets very angry and depressed, and cuts herself. Jane has a similar pattern with her family, where she cycles between loving them and desiring closeness and then feeling betrayed and abandoned when they disappoint her.

- **Symptoms:** Mood lability, self-harm (cutting), and relationship instability

- **Client's goals for therapy:** Jane wants to find strategies for regulating her emotions and improving her relationships.

- **Attitude toward therapy:** Jane was in therapy before, which was helpful until the therapist disappointed Jane by going on vacation during a time she needed support, after which Jane felt betrayed and abandoned and quit therapy. Jane is worried that you (her new therapist) may betray or abandon her just like her previous therapist.

- **Strengths:** When Jane is emotionally regulated, she is able to reflect on her emotions and work collaboratively with her therapist.

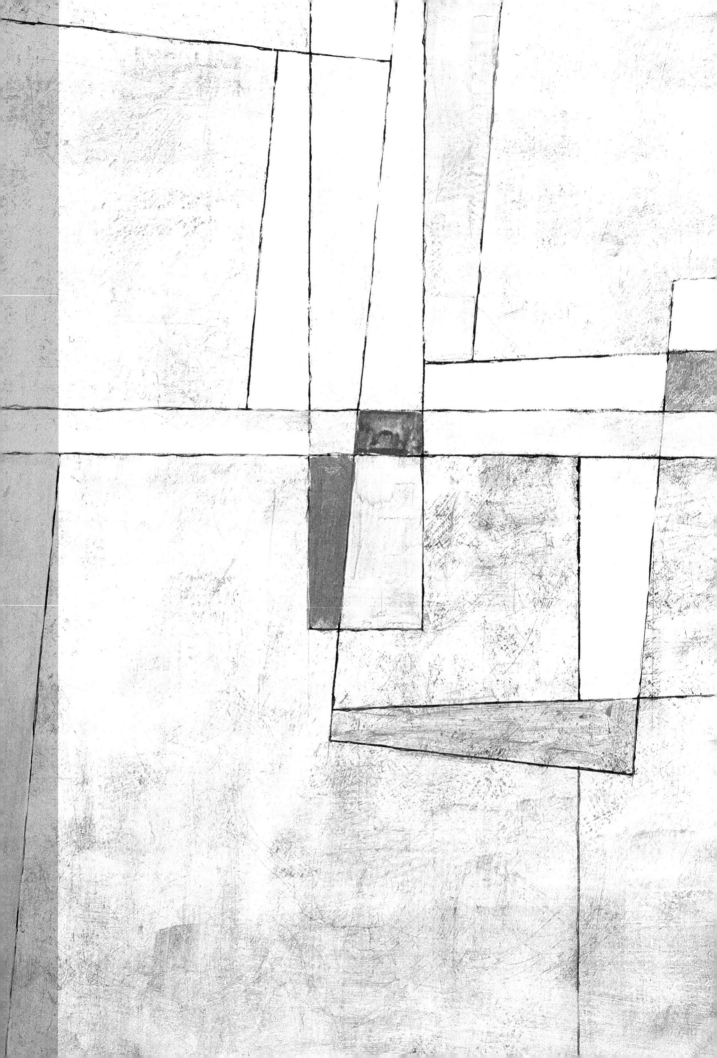

Strategies for Enhancing the Deliberate Practice Exercises

Part III consists of one chapter, Chapter 3, that provides additional advice and instructions for trainers and trainees so that they can reap more benefits from the deliberate practice exercises in Part II. Chapter 3 offers six key points for getting the most out of deliberate practice, guidelines for practicing appropriately responsive treatment, evaluation strategies, methods for ensuring trainee well-being and respecting their privacy, and advice for monitoring the trainer–trainee relationship.

How to Get the Most Out of Deliberate Practice: Additional Guidance for Trainers and Trainees

In Chapter 2 and in the exercises themselves, we provided instructions for completing these deliberate practice exercises. This chapter provides guidance on big-picture topics that trainers will need to successfully integrate deliberate practice into their training program. This guidance is based on relevant research and the experiences and feedback from trainers at over a dozen psychotherapy training programs who volunteered to test the deliberate practice exercises in this book. We cover topics including evaluation, getting the most from deliberate practice, trainee well-being, respecting trainee privacy, trainer self-evaluation, responsive treatment, and the trainee-trainer alliance.

Six Key Points for Getting the Most From Deliberate Practice

Following are six key points of advice for trainers and trainees to get the most benefits from the dialectical behavior therapy (DBT) deliberate practice exercises. The following advice is gleaned from experiences vetting and practicing the exercises, sometimes in different languages, with many trainees across many countries, on different occasions.

Key Point 1: Create Realistic Emotional Stimuli

A key component of deliberate practice is using stimuli that provoke similar reactions to challenging real-life work settings. For example, pilots train with flight simulators that present mechanical failures and dangerous weather conditions; surgeons practice with surgical simulators that present medical complications with only seconds to respond. Training with challenging stimuli will increase trainees' capacity to perform therapy effectively under stress—for example, with clients they find challenging. The stimuli used for DBT deliberate practice exercises are role-plays of challenging client statements in therapy. **It is important that the trainee who is role-playing the client perform the script with appropriate emotional expression and maintain eye contact with the**

https://doi.org/10.1037/0000322-017

Deliberate Practice in Dialectical Behavior Therapy, by T. Boritz, S. McMain, A. Vaz, and T. Rousmaniere

therapist. For example, if the client statement calls for sad emotion, the trainee should try to express sadness eye-to-eye with the therapist. We offer the following suggestions regarding emotional expressiveness:

1. The emotional tone of the role-play matters more than the exact words of each script. Trainees role-playing the client should feel free to improvise and change the words if it will help them be more emotionally expressive. Trainees do not need to stick 100% exactly to the script. In fact, to read off the script during the exercise can sound flat and prohibit eye contact. Rather, trainees in the client role should first read the client statement silently to themselves then, when ready, say it in an emotional manner while looking directly at the trainee playing the therapist. This will help the experience feel more real and engaging for the therapist.

2. Trainees whose first language is not English may particularly benefit from reviewing and changing the words in the client statement script before each role-play so they can find words that feel congruent and facilitate emotional expression.

3. Trainees role-playing the client should try to use tonal and nonverbal expressions of feelings. For example, if a script calls for anger, the trainee can speak with an angry voice and make fists with their hands; if a script calls for shame or guilt, the trainee could hunch over and wince; if a script calls for sadness, the trainee could speak in a soft or deflated voice.

4. If trainees are having persistent difficulties acting believably when following a particular script in the role of client, it may help to first do a "demo round" by reading directly from paper and then, immediately after, dropping the paper to make eye contact and repeating the same client statement from memory. Some trainees reported that this helped them "become available as a real client" and made the role-play feel less artificial. Some trainees did three or four "demo rounds" to get fully into their role as a client.

Key Point 2: Customize the Exercises to Fit Your Unique Training Circumstances

Deliberate practice is less about adhering to specific *rules* than it is about using *training principles*. Every trainer has their own individual teaching style and every trainee their own learning process. Thus, the exercises in this book are designed to be flexibly customized by trainers across different training contexts within different cultures. Trainees and trainers are encouraged to continually adjust exercises to optimize their practice. The most effective training will occur when deliberate practice exercises are customized to fit the learning needs of each trainee and culture of each training site. In our experience with many trainers and trainees across many countries, we found that everyone spontaneously customized the exercises for their unique training circumstances. No two trainers followed the exact same procedure. Here are a few examples:

- One supervisor used the exercises with a trainee who found all the client statements to be too hard, including the "beginner" stimuli. This trainee had multiple reactions in the "too hard" category on the Deliberate Practice Reaction Form in Appendix A, including nausea, severe shame, and self-doubt. The trainee disclosed to the supervisor that she had experienced extremely harsh learning environments earlier in her life and found the role-plays to be highly evocative. To help, the supervisor followed the suggestions offered in Appendix A to make the stimuli progressively easier until the trainee reported feeling a "good challenge" on the Deliberate Practice Reaction Form. Over many weeks of practice, the trainee developed a sense of safety and was able to practice with more difficult client statements. (Note that if the supervisor had proceeded at the too hard difficulty level, the trainee might have complied while hiding her negative reactions, become emotionally dysregulated and overwhelmed, leading to shame and subsequent withdrawal, and thus prohibiting her skill development and risking dropout from training.)

- Supervisors of trainees for whom English was not their first language adjusted the client statements to their own primary language.

- One supervisor used the exercises with a trainee who found all the stimuli to be too easy, including the advanced client statements. This supervisor quickly moved to improvising more challenging client statements from scratch by following the instructions in Appendix A on how to make client statements more challenging.

Key Point 3: Discover Your Own Unique Personal Therapeutic Style

Deliberate practice in psychotherapy can be likened to the process of learning to play jazz music. Every jazz musician prides themselves in their skillful improvisations, and the process of "finding your own voice" is a prerequisite for expertise in jazz musicianship. Yet improvisations are not a collection of random notes but the culmination of extensive deliberate practice over time. Indeed, the ability to improvise is built on many hours of dedicated practice of scales, melodies, harmonies, and so on. Much in the same way, psychotherapy trainees are encouraged to experience the scripted interventions in this book not as ends in themselves but as a means to promote skill in a systematic fashion. Over time, effective therapeutic creativity can be aided, instead of constrained, by dedicated practice in these therapeutic "melodies."

Key Point 4: Engage in a Sufficient Amount of Rehearsal

Deliberate practice uses rehearsal to move skills into procedural memory, which helps trainees maintain access to skills even when working with challenging clients. This only works if trainees engage in many repetitions of the exercises. Think of a challenging sport or musical instrument you learned: How many rehearsals would a professional need to feel confident performing a new skill? Psychotherapy is no easier than those other fields!

Key Point 5: Continually Adjust Difficulty

A crucial element of deliberate practice is training at an optimal difficulty level: neither too easy nor too hard. To achieve this, do difficulty assessments and adjustments with the Deliberate Practice Reaction Form in Appendix A. **Do not skip this step!** If trainees don't feel any of the "good challenge" reactions at the bottom of the Deliberate Practice Reaction Form, then the exercise is probably too easy; if they feel any of the "too hard" reactions, then the exercise could be too difficult for the trainee to benefit. Advanced trainees and therapists may find all the client statements too easy. If so, they should follow the instructions in Appendix A on making client statements harder to make the role-plays sufficiently challenging.

Key Point 6: Putting It All Together With the Practice Transcript and Mock Therapy Sessions

Some trainees may feel a further need for greater contextualization of the individual therapy responses associated with each skill, feeling the need to integrate the disparate pieces of their training in a more coherent manner, with a simulation that mimics a real therapy session. The annotated transcript in Exercise 13 and the mock therapy sessions in Exercise 14 give trainees this opportunity, allowing them to practice delivering different responses sequentially in a more realistic therapeutic encounter.

Responsive Treatment

The exercises in this book are designed not only to help trainees acquire specific skills of DBT but to use them in ways that are responsive to each individual client and their context and are driven by a solid case formulation (Boritz et al., 2021, 2023; McMain et al., 2019). Across the psychotherapy literature, this stance has been referred to as *appropriate responsiveness*, wherein the therapists exercise flexible judgment, based in their perception of the client's emotional state, needs, and goals, and integrates techniques and other interpersonal skills in pursuit of optimal client outcomes (Hatcher, 2015; Stiles et al., 1998). The effective therapist is responsive to the emerging context. As Stiles and Horvath (2017) argued, a therapist is effective because they are appropriately responsive. Doing the "right thing" may be different each time and means providing each client with an individually tailored response.

Appropriate responsiveness counters a misconception that deliberate practice rehearsal is designed to promote robotic repetition of therapy techniques. Psychotherapy researchers have shown that overadherence to a particular model while neglecting client preferences reduces therapy effectiveness (e.g., Castonguay et al., 1996; Henry et al., 1993; Owen & Hilsenroth, 2014). Therapist flexibility, on the other hand, has been shown to improve outcomes (e.g., Bugatti & Boswell, 2016; Kendall & Beidas, 2007; Kendall & Frank, 2018). It is important, therefore, that trainees practice their newly learned skills in a manner that is flexible and responsive to the unique needs of a diverse range of clients (Hatcher, 2015; Hill & Knox, 2013). It is thus of paramount importance for trainees to develop the necessary perceptual skills to be able to attune to what the client is experiencing in the moment and form their response based on the client moment by moment context.

The supervisor must help the supervisee to specifically attune themselves to the unique and specific needs of the clients during sessions. By enacting responsiveness with the supervisee, the supervisor can demonstrate its value and make it more explicit. In these ways, attention can be given to the larger picture of appropriate responsiveness. Here the trainee and supervisor can work together to help the trainee master not just the techniques, but how therapists can use their judgment to put the techniques together to foster positive change. Helping trainees keep this overarching goal in mind while reviewing therapy sessions is a valuable feature of supervision that is difficult to obtain otherwise (Hatcher, 2015).

It is also important that deliberate practice occurs within a context of broader DBT training. The DBT supervision model takes into account the inherently challenging nature of the therapeutic work with the client populations DBT is typically applied to (Waltz et al., 1998). As noted in Chapter 1, training should be combined with theoretical learning and observation of competent DBT psychotherapists, as well as personal therapeutic work with clients. Trainees learning DBT generally receive individual supervision that includes some form of observation (e.g., audio, videotape, or live supervision). In addition, the DBT model encourages therapists at all stages of learning to participate on a consultation team, as doing the therapy effectively with complex client populations is near to impossible without the support and guidance of a consultation team. When the trainer or trainee determines that the trainee is having difficulty acquiring DBT skills, it is important to carefully assess what is missing or needed. Assessment can then lead to the appropriate solution, as the trainer and trainee collaboratively determine what is needed to solve the identified problem (similar to how we might approach solution analysis with a DBT client).

Being Mindful of Trainee Well-Being

Although negative effects that some clients experience in psychotherapy have been well documented (Barlow, 2010), negative effects of training and supervision on trainees has received less attention (Ellis et al., 2014). DBT supervision, like the treatment itself, aims to create an accepting and safe context that encourages and supports the trainee in delivering the most effective treatment possible (Fruzzetti et al., 1997). A general approach to DBT supervision is to try to achieve and maintain the fundamental dialectical balance between acceptance and change. The supervisor does this by working to understand and validate the supervisee's experience. At the same time, the supervisor may function as a coach, giving directions, providing feedback on performance, and encouraging the therapist to persist at trying difficult things (Waltz et al., 1998).

To support strong self-efficacy, trainers must ensure that trainees are practicing at a correct difficulty level. The exercises in this book feature guidance for frequently assessing and adjusting the difficulty level, so trainees can rehearse at a level that precisely targets their personal skill threshold. Trainers and supervisors must be mindful to provide an appropriate challenge. One risk to trainees that is particularly pertinent to this book occurs when using role-plays that are too difficult. The Deliberate Practice Reaction Form in Appendix A is provided to help trainers ensure that role-plays are done at an appropriate challenge level. Trainers or trainees may be tempted to skip the difficulty assessments and adjustments, out of their motivation to focus on rehearsal to make fast progress and quickly acquire skills. But across all our test sites, we found that skipping the difficulty assessments and adjustments caused more problems and hindered skill acquisition more than any other error. Thus, trainers are advised to remember that **one of their most important responsibilities is to remind trainees to do the difficulty assessments and adjustments.**

Additionally, the Reaction Form serves a dual purpose of helping trainees develop the important skills of self-monitoring and self-awareness (Bennett-Levy & Finlay-Jones, 2018). This will help trainees adopt a positive and empowered stance regarding their own self-care and should facilitate career-long professional development.

Respecting Trainee Privacy

The deliberate practice exercises in this book may stir up complex or uncomfortable personal reactions within trainees, including, for example, memories of past traumas. Exploring psychological and emotional reactions may make some trainees feel vulnerable. Therapists of every career stage, from trainees to seasoned therapists with decades of experience, commonly experience shame, embarrassment, and self-doubt in this process. Although these experiences can be valuable for building trainees' self-awareness, it is important that training remain focused on professional skill development and not blur into personal therapy (e.g., Ellis et al., 2014). Therefore, one trainer role is to remind trainees to maintain appropriate boundaries.

Trainees must have the final say about what to disclose or not disclose to their trainer. Trainees should keep in mind that the goal is for the trainee to expand their own self-awareness and psychological capacity to stay active and helpful while experiencing uncomfortable reactions. The trainer does not need to know the specific details about the trainee's inner world for this to happen.

Trainees should be instructed to share only personal information that they feel comfortable sharing. The Reaction Form and difficulty assessment process are designed to help trainees build their self-awareness while retaining control over their privacy. Trainees can be reminded that the goal is for them to learn about their own inner world. They do not necessarily have to share that information with trainers or peers (Bennett-Levy & Finlay-Jones, 2018). Likewise, trainees should be instructed to respect the confidentiality of their peers.

Trainer Self-Evaluation

The exercises in this book were tested at a wide range of training sites around the world, including graduate courses, practicum sites, and private practice offices. Although trainers reported that the exercises were highly effective for training, some also said that they felt disoriented by how different deliberate practice feels compared with their traditional methods of clinical education. Many felt comfortable evaluating their trainees' performance but were less sure about their own performance as trainers.

The most common concern we heard from trainers was, "My trainees are doing great, but I'm not sure if I am doing this correctly!" To address this concern, we recommend trainers perform periodic self-evaluations using the following five criteria:

1. Observe trainees' work performance.
2. Provide continual corrective feedback.
3. Ensure rehearsal of specific skills is just beyond the trainees' current ability.
4. Ensure that the trainee is practicing at the right difficulty level (neither too easy nor too challenging).
5. Continuously assess trainee performance with real clients.

Criterion 1: Observe Trainees' Work Performance

Determining how well we are doing as trainers means first having valid information about how well trainees are responding to training. This requires that we directly observe trainees practicing skills to provide corrective feedback and evaluation. One risk of deliberate practice is that trainees gain competence in performing therapy skills in role-plays but those skills do not transfer to trainees' work with real clients. Thus, trainers will ideally also have the opportunity to observe samples of trainees' work with real clients, either live or via recorded video. Supervisors and consultants rely heavily—and, too often, exclusively—on supervisees' and consultees' narrative accounts of their work with clients (Goodyear & Nelson, 1997). Haggerty and Hilsenroth (2011) described this challenge:

> Suppose a loved one has to undergo surgery and you need to choose between two surgeons, one of whom has never been directly observed by an experienced surgeon while performing any surgery. He or she would perform the

surgery and return to his or her attending physician and try to recall, some-times incompletely or inaccurately, the intricate steps of the surgery they just performed. It is hard to imagine that anyone, given a choice, would prefer this over a professional who has been routinely observed in the practice of their craft. (p. 193)

Criterion 2: Provide Continual Corrective Feedback

Trainees need corrective feedback to learn what they are doing well, what they are doing poorly, and how to improve their skills. Feedback should be as specific and incre-mental as possible. Examples of specific feedback are, "Your voice sounds rushed. Try slowing down by pausing for a few seconds between your statements to the client," and, "That's excellent how you are making eye contact with the client." Examples of vague and nonspecific feedback are, "Try to build better rapport with the client," and, "Try to be more open to the client's feelings."

Criterion 3: Specific Skill Rehearsal Just Beyond the Trainees' Current Ability (Zone of Proximal Development)

Deliberate practice emphasizes skill acquisition via behavioral rehearsal. Trainers should endeavor not to get caught up in client conceptualization at the expense of focusing on skills. For many trainers, this requires significant discipline and self-restraint. It is simply more enjoyable to talk about psychotherapy theory (e.g., case conceptualization, treatment planning, nuances of psychotherapy models, similar cases the supervisor has had) than watch trainees rehearse skills. Trainees have many questions and supervisors have an abundance of experience; the allotted supervision time can easily be filled by sharing knowledge. The supervisor gets to sound smart, while the trainee doesn't have to struggle with acquiring skills at their learning edge. While answering questions is important, trainees' intellectual knowledge about psychotherapy can quickly surpass their procedural ability to perform psychotherapy, particularly with clients they find challenging. Here's a simple rule of thumb: The trainer provides the knowledge, but the behavioral rehearsal provides the skill (Rousmaniere, 2019).

Criterion 4: Practice at the Right Difficulty Level (Neither Too Easy nor Too Challenging)

Deliberate practice involves *optimal strain*: practicing skills just beyond the trainee's current skill threshold so they can learn incrementally without becoming overwhelmed (Ericsson, 2006). Trainers should use difficulty assessments and adjustments throughout deliberate practice to ensure that trainees are practicing at the right difficulty level. Note that some trainees are surprised by their unpleasant reactions to exercises (e.g., disassociation, nausea, blanking out) and may be tempted to "push through" exercises that are too hard. This can happen out of fear of failing a course, fear of being judged as incompetent, or negative self-impressions by the trainee (e.g., "This shouldn't be so hard"). Trainers should normalize the fact that there will be wide variation in perceived difficulty of the exercises and encourage trainees to respect their own personal training process.

Criterion 5: Continuously Assess Trainee Performance With Real Clients

The goal of deliberately practicing psychotherapy skills is to improve trainees' effec-tiveness at helping real clients. One of the risks in deliberate practice training is that the benefits will not generalize: Trainees' acquired competence in specific skills may not translate into work with real clients. Thus, it is important that trainers assess the impact of deliberate practice on trainees' work with real clients. Ideally, this is done through triangulation of multiple data points:

1. Client data (verbal self-report and routine outcome monitoring data)
2. Supervisor's report
3. Trainee's self-report

If the trainee's effectiveness with real clients is not improving after deliberate practice, the trainer should do a careful assessment of the difficulty. If the supervisor or trainer feels it is a skill acquisition issues, they may want to consider adjusting the deliberate practice routine to better suit the trainee's learning needs and/or style.

Therapists have traditionally been evaluated from a lens of *process accountability* (Markman & Tetlock, 2000; see also Goodyear, 2015), which focuses on demonstrating specific behaviors (e.g., fidelity to a treatment model) without regard to the impact on clients. We propose that clinical effectiveness is better assessed through a lens tightly focused on client outcomes and that learning objectives shift from performing behaviors that experts have decided are effective (i.e., the competence model) to highly individualized behavioral goals tailored to each trainee's zone of proximal development and performance feedback. This model of assessment has been termed *outcome accountability* (Goodyear, 2015), which focuses on client changes, rather than therapist competence, independent of how the therapist might be performing expected tasks.

Guidance for Trainees

The central theme of this book has been that skill rehearsal is not automatically helpful. Deliberate practice must be done well for trainees to benefit (Ericsson & Pool, 2016). In this chapter and in the exercises, we offer guidance for effective deliberate practice. We would also like to provide additional advice specifically for trainees. That advice is drawn from what we have learned at our volunteer deliberate practice test sites around the world. We cover how to discover your own training process, active effort, playfulness and taking breaks during deliberate practice, your right to control your self-disclosure to trainers, monitoring training results, monitoring complex reactions toward the trainer, and your own personal therapy.

Individualized DBT Training: Finding Your Zone of Proximal Development

Deliberate practice works best when training targets each trainee's personal skill thresholds. Also termed the *zone of proximal development*, a term first coined by Vygotsky in reference to developmental learning theory (Zaretskii, 2009), this is the area just beyond the trainee's current ability, but which is possible to reach with the assistance of a teacher or coach (Wass & Golding, 2014). **If a deliberate practice exercise is either too easy or too hard, the trainee will not benefit.** To maximize training productivity, elite performers follow a "challenging but not overwhelming" principle: Tasks that are too far beyond their capacity will prove ineffective and even harmful; it is equally true that mindlessly repeating what they already can do confidently will prove equally fruitless. Because of this, deliberate practice requires ongoing assessment of the trainee's current skill and concurrent difficulty adjustment to consistently target a "good enough" challenge. Thus, if you are practicing Exercise 11, "Promoting Dialectical Thinking Through Both–And Statements" and it just feels too difficult, consider moving back to a more comfortable skill, such as validation (Exercise 2) or problem assessment (Exercise 4), that you may feel you have already mastered.

Active Effort

It is important for trainees to maintain an active and sustained effort while doing the deliberate practice exercises in this book. Deliberate practice helps when trainees push themselves up to and past their current ability. This is best achieved when trainees take ownership of their own practice by guiding their training partners to adjust role-plays to be as high on the difficulty scale as possible without hurting themselves. This will look different for every trainee. Although it can feel uncomfortable or even frightening, this is the zone of proximal development where the most gains can be made. Simply reading and repeating the written scripts will provide little or no benefit. Trainees are advised to remember that their effort from training should lead to more confidence and comfort in session with real clients.

Stay the Course: Effort Versus Flow

Deliberate practice only works if trainees push themselves hard enough to break out of their old patterns of performance, which then permits growth of new skills (Ericsson & Pool, 2016). Because deliberate practice constantly focuses on the current edge of one's performance capacity, it is inevitably a straining endeavor. Indeed, professionals are unlikely to make lasting performance improvements unless there is sufficient engagement in tasks that are just at the edge of one's current capacity (Ericsson, 2003, 2006). From athletics or fitness training, many of us are familiar with this process of being pushed out of our comfort zones, followed by adaptation. The same process applies to our mental and emotional abilities.

Many trainees might feel surprised to discover that deliberate practice for DBT feels harder than psychotherapy with a real client. This may be because when working with a real client, a therapist can get into a state of *flow* (Csikszentmihalyi, 1997), where work feels effortless. It is not uncommon for beginner DBT trainees to feel more comfortable with either validation strategies or change strategies: It is difficult at the beginning to focus continually on balancing acceptance and change. At times, DBT trainees may feel overwhelmed by the task of weaving these strategies seamlessly, and this can lead to feelings of ineffectiveness. In such cases, DBT trainees can consider returning temporarily to offering response formats with which they are more familiar and feel more proficient (e.g., focusing simply on providing validating), to increase a sense of confidence and mastery before trying once again to practice more complex skills.

Discover Your Own Training Process

The effectiveness of deliberate practice is directly related to the effort and ownership trainees exert while doing the exercises. Trainers can provide guidance, but it is important for trainees to learn about their own idiosyncratic training processes over time. This will let them become masters of their own training and prepare for a career-long process of professional development. The following are a few examples of personal training processes trainees discovered while engaging in deliberate practice:

- One trainee noticed that she is good at persisting while an exercise is challenging but also that she requires more rehearsal than other trainees to feel comfortable with a new skill. This trainee focused on developing patience with her own pace of progress.

- One trainee noticed that he could acquire new skills rather quickly, with only a few repetitions. However, he also noticed that his reactions to evocative client statements could jump very quickly and unpredictably from the "good challenge" to "too hard" categories, so he needed to carefully attend to the reactions listed in the Deliberate Practice Reaction Form.

- One trainee described herself as "perfectionistic" and felt a strong urge to "push through" an exercise even when she had anxiety reactions in the "too hard" category, such as nausea and disassociation. This caused the trainee not to benefit from the exercises and risk getting demoralized. This trainee focused on going slower, developing self-compassion regarding her anxiety reactions, and asking her training partners to make role-plays less challenging.

Trainees are encouraged to reflect deeply on their own experiences using the exercises to learn the most about themselves and their personal learning processes.

Playfulness and Taking Breaks

Psychotherapy is serious work that often involves painful feelings. However, practicing psychotherapy can be playful and fun (Scott Miller, personal communication, 2017). Trainees should remember that one of the main goals of deliberate practice is to experiment with different approaches and styles of therapy. If deliberate practice ever feels rote, boring, or routine, it probably isn't going to help advance trainees' skill. In this case, trainees should try to liven it up. A good way to do this is to introduce an atmosphere of playfulness. For example, trainees can do the following:

- Use different vocal tones, speech pacing, body gestures, or other languages. This can expand trainees' communication range.

- Practice while standing up or walking around outside. This can help trainees get new perspectives on the process of therapy.

The supervisor can also ask trainees if they would like to take a 5- to 10-minute break between questions, particularly if the trainees are dealing with difficult emotions and are feeling overwhelmed or stressed out.

Additional Deliberate Practice Opportunities

This book focuses on deliberate practice methods that involve active, live engagement between trainees and a supervisor. Importantly, deliberate practice can extend beyond these focused training sessions and be used for homework. For example, a trainee might read the client stimuli quietly or aloud and practice their responses independently between sessions with a supervisor. In such cases, it is important for the trainee to say their therapist responses aloud, rather than rehearse silently in one's head. Alternatively, two trainees can practice as a pair, without the supervisor. Although the absence of a supervisor limits one source of feedback, the peer trainee who is playing the client can perform this role, as they can when a supervisor is present. Importantly, these additional deliberate practice opportunities are intended to take place between focused training sessions with a supervisor. To optimize the quality of the deliberate practice when conducted independently or without a supervisor, we have developed a Deliberate Practice Diary Form that can be found in Appendix B or downloaded from https://www.apa.org/pubs/books/deliberate-practice-dialectical-behavior-therapy (see the "Clinician and Practitioner Resources" tab). This form provides a template for the trainee to record their experience of the deliberate practice activity, and, ideally, it will aid in the consolidation of learning. This form can be used as part of the evaluation process with the supervisor, but it is not necessarily intended for that purpose, and trainees are certainly welcome to bring their experience with the independent practice into the next meeting with the supervisor.

Monitoring Training Results

While trainers will evaluate trainees using a competency-focused model, trainees are also encouraged to take ownership of their own training process and look for results of deliberate practice themselves. Trainees should experience the results of deliberate practice within a few training sessions. A lack of results can be demoralizing for trainees and can result in trainees applying less effort and focus in deliberate practice. Trainees who are not seeing results should openly discuss this problem with their trainer and experiment with adjusting their deliberate practice process. Results can include client outcomes and improving the trainee's own work as a therapist, their personal development, and their overall training.

Client Outcomes

The most important result of deliberate practice is an improvement in trainees' client outcomes. This can be assessed via routine outcome measurement (Lambert, 2010; Prescott et al., 2017), qualitative data (McLeod, 2017), and informal discussions with clients. However, trainees should note that an improvement in client outcome due to deliberate practice can sometimes be challenging to achieve quickly, given that the largest amount of variance in client outcome is due to client variables (Bohart & Wade, 2013). For example, a client with severe chronic symptoms may not respond quickly to any treatment, regardless of how effectively a trainee practices. For some clients, an increase in patience and self-compassion regarding their symptoms, rather than an immediate decrease in symptoms, may be a sign of progress. Thus, trainees are advised to keep their expectations for client change realistic in the context of their client's symptoms, history, and presentation. It is important that trainees do not try to force their clients to improve in therapy for the trainee to feel like they are making progress in their training (Rousmaniere, 2016).

Trainee's Work as a Therapist

One important result of deliberate practice is change within the trainee regarding their work with clients. For example, trainees at test sites reported feeling more comfortable sitting with evocative clients, more confident addressing uncomfortable topics in therapy, and more responsive to a broader range of clients.

Trainee's Personal Development

Another important result of deliberate practice is personal growth within the trainee. For example, trainees at test sites reported becoming more in touch with their own feelings, increased self-compassion, and enhanced motivation to work with a broader range of clients.

Trainee's Training Process

Another valuable result of deliberate practice is improvement in the trainees' training process. For example, trainees at test sites reported becoming more aware of their personal training style, preferences, strengths, and challenges. Over time, trainees should grow to feel more ownership of their training process. Training to be a psychotherapist is a complex process that occurs over many years. Experienced, expert therapists still report continuing to grow well beyond their graduate school years (Orlinsky et al., 2005). Furthermore, training is not a linear process. It is not uncommon for psychotherapists to feel they have mastered a set of skills with one client, only to be confronted with new challenges and the need for further skill development with different clients or in different clinical situations.

The Trainee–Trainer Alliance: Monitoring Complex Reactions Toward the Trainer

Trainees who engage in hard deliberate practice often report experiencing complex feelings towards their trainer. For example, one trainee said, "I know this is helping, but I also don't look forward to it!" Another trainee reported feeling both appreciation and frustration simultaneously toward her trainer. Trainees are advised to remember intensive training they have done in other fields, such as athletics or music. When a coach pushes a trainee to the edge of their ability, it is common for trainees to have complex reactions toward them.

This does not necessarily mean that the trainer is doing anything wrong. In fact, intensive training inevitably stirs up reactions toward the trainer, such as frustration, annoyance, disappointment, or anger, that coexist with the appreciation they feel. In fact, if trainees do not experience complex reactions, it is worth considering whether the deliberate practice is sufficiently challenging. But what we asserted earlier about rights to privacy apply here as well. Because professional mental health training is hierarchical and evaluative, trainers should not require or even expect trainees to share complex reactions they may be experiencing toward them. Trainers should stay open to their sharing, but the choice always remains with the trainee.

Trainee's Own Therapy

When engaging in deliberate practice, many trainees discover aspects of their inner world that may benefit from attending their own psychotherapy. For example, one trainee discovered that her clients' anger stirred up her own painful memories of abuse, another trainee found himself dissociating while practicing information exposure to emotions, and another trainee experienced overwhelming shame and self-judgment when she couldn't master skills after just a few repetitions.

Although these discoveries were unnerving at first, they were ultimately beneficial because they motivated the trainees to seek out their own therapy. Many therapists attend their own therapy. In fact, Norcross and Guy (2005) found in their review of 17 studies that about 75% of the more than 8,000 therapist participants have attended their own therapy. Orlinsky et al. (2005) found that more than 90% of therapists who attended their own therapy reported it as helpful.

QUESTIONS FOR TRAINEES

1. Are you balancing the effort to improve your skills with patience and self-compassion for your learning process?
2. Are you attending to any shame or self-judgment that arising from training?
3. Are you being mindful of your personal boundaries and also respecting any complex feelings you may have toward your trainers?

Difficulty Assessments and Adjustments

Deliberate practice works best if the exercises are performed at a good challenge that is neither too hard nor too easy. To ensure that they are practicing at the correct difficulty, trainees should do a difficulty assessment and adjustment after each level of client statement is completed (beginner, intermediate, and advanced). To do this, use the following instructions and the Deliberate Practice Reaction Form (Figure A.1), which is also available in the "Clinician and Practitioner Resources" tab at https://www.apa.org/pubs/books/deliberate-practice-dialectical-behavior-therapy. **Do not skip this process!**

How to Assess Difficulty

The therapist completes the Deliberate Practice Reaction Form (Figure A.1). If they

- rate the difficulty of the exercise above an 8 or had any of the reactions in the "Too Hard" column, follow the instructions to make the exercise easier;

- rate the difficulty of the exercise below a 4 or didn't have any of the reactions in the "Good Challenge" column, proceed to the next level of harder client statements or follow the instructions to make exercise harder; or

- rate the difficulty of the exercise between 4 and 8 and have at least one reaction in the "Good Challenge" column, do not proceed to the harder client statements but rather repeat the same level.

Making Client Statements Easier

If the therapist ever rates the difficulty of the exercise above an 8 or has any of the reactions in the "Too Hard" column, use the next level easier client statements (e.g., if you were using advanced client statements, switch to intermediate). But if you already were using beginner client statements, use the following methods to make the client statements even easier:

- The person playing the client can use the same beginner client statements but this time in a softer, calmer voice and with a smile. This softens the emotional tone.

FIGURE A.1. Deliberate Practice Reaction Form

Question 1: How challenging was it to fulfill the skill criteria for this exercise?

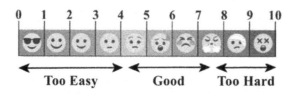

Question 2: Did you have any reactions in "good challenge" or "too hard" categories? (yes/no)					
Good Challenge			Too Hard		
Emotions and Thoughts	Body Reactions	Urges	Emotions and Thoughts	Body Reactions	Urges
Manageable shame, self-judgment, irritation, anger, sadness, etc.	Body tension, sighs, shallow breathing, increased heart rate, warmth, dry mouth	Looking away, withdrawing, changing focus	Severe or overwhelming shame, self-judgment, rage, grief, guilt, etc.	Migraines, dizziness, foggy thinking, diarrhea, disassociation, numbness, blanking out, nausea, etc.	Shutting down, giving up

Too Easy	Good Challenge	Too Hard
⬇	⬇	⬇
Proceed to next difficulty level	Repeat the same difficulty level	Go back to previous difficulty level

Note. Reprinted from *Deliberate Practice in Emotion-Focused Therapy* (p. 180), by R. N. Goldman, A. Vaz, and T. Rousmaniere, 2021, American Psychological Association (https://doi.org/10.1037/0000227-000). Copyright 2021 by the American Psychological Association.

- The client can improvise with topics that are less evocative or make the therapist more comfortable, such as talking about topics without expressing feelings, the future/past (avoiding the here and now), or any topic outside therapy (see Figure A.2).

- The therapist can take a short break (5–10 minutes) between questions.

- The trainer can expand the "feedback phase" by discussing dialectical behavior therapy or psychotherapy theory and research. This should shift the trainees' focus toward more detached or intellectual topics and reduce the emotional intensity.

Making Client Statements Harder

If the therapist rates the difficulty of the exercise below a 4 or didn't have any of the reactions in the "Good Challenge" column, proceed to next level harder client statements. If you were already using the advanced client statements, the client should make the exercise even harder, using the following guidelines:

FIGURE A.2. How to Make Client Statements Easier or Harder in Role-Plays

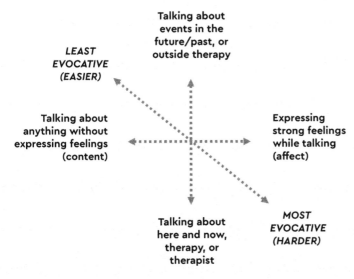

Talking about events in the future/past, or outside therapy

LEAST EVOCATIVE (EASIER)

Talking about anything without expressing feelings (content)

Expressing strong feelings while talking (affect)

Talking about here and now, therapy, or therapist

MOST EVOCATIVE (HARDER)

Note. Figure created by Jason Whipple, PhD.

- The person playing the client can use the advanced client statements again with a more distressed voice (e.g., very angry, sad, sarcastic) or unpleasant facial expression. This should increase the emotional tone.

- The client can improvise new client statements with topics that are more evocative or make the therapist uncomfortable, such as expressing strong feelings or talking about the here and now, therapy, or the therapist (see Figure A.2).

Note. The purpose of a deliberate practice session is not to get through all the client statements and therapist responses but rather to spend as much time as possible practicing at the correct difficulty level. This may mean that trainees repeat the same statements or responses many times, which is OK, as long as the difficulty remains at the "good challenge" level.

Deliberate Practice Diary Form

This book focuses on deliberate practice methods that involve active, live engagement between trainees and a supervisor. Importantly, deliberate practice can extend beyond these focused training sessions. For example, a trainee might read the client stimuli quietly or aloud and practice their responses independently between sessions with a supervisor. In such cases, it is important for the trainee to speak aloud rather than rehearse silently in one's head. Alternatively, two trainees can practice without the supervisor. Although the absence of a supervisor limits one source of feedback, the peer trainee who is playing the client can serve this role, as they can when a supervisor is present. Importantly, these additional deliberate practice opportunities are intended to take place between focused training sessions with a supervisor. To optimize the quality of the deliberate practice when conducted independently or without a supervisor, we have developed a Deliberate Practice Diary Form that can also be downloaded from the "Clinician and Practitioner Resources" tab at https://www.apa.org/pubs/books/deliberate-practice-dialectical-behavior-therapy. This form provides a template for the trainee to record their experience of the deliberate practice activity and, hopefully, will aid in the consolidation of learning. This form can also be used as part of the evaluation process with the supervisor but is not necessarily intended for that purpose, and trainees are certainly welcome to bring their experience with the independent practice into the next meeting with the supervisor.

Deliberate Practice Diary Form

Use this form to consolidate learnings from the deliberate practice exercises. Please protect your personal boundaries by only sharing information that you are comfortable disclosing.

Name: _____ Date: _____

Exercise: _____

Question 1. What was helpful or worked well this deliberate practice session? In what way?

Question 2. What was unhelpful or didn't go well this deliberate practice session? In what way?

Question 3. What did you learn about yourself, your current skills, and skills you'd like to keep improving? Feel free to share any details, but only those you are comfortable disclosing.

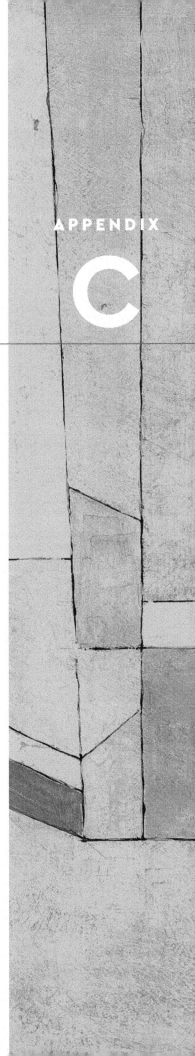

Sample Dialectical Behavior Therapy Syllabus With Embedded Deliberate Practice Exercises

This appendix provides a sample one-semester, three-unit course dedicated to teaching dialectical behavior therapy (DBT). This course is appropriate for graduate students (masters and doctoral) at all levels of training, including first-year students who have not yet worked with clients. If offering a full DBT course is not possible, aspects of the syllabus and associated exercises can be adapted for use in other courses, practica, didactic training events at externships and internships, workshops, and continuing education for postgraduate therapists.

Course Title: Dialectical Behavior Therapy: Theory, Case Formulation, and Deliberate Practice

Course Description

This course teaches theory, principles, and core clinical skills of DBT. As a course with both didactic and practicum elements, it will review the theory and research on DBT, frameworks used to formulate and understand client problems, and the use of deliberate practice to enable students to acquire 12 key DBT skills.

Course Objectives

Students who complete this course will be able to do the following:

1. Describe the core theory, research, and skills of DBT
2. Apply the principles of deliberate practice for career-long clinical skill development
3. Demonstrate key DBT skills
4. Evaluate how they can fit DBT skills into their developing therapeutic framework
5. Employ DBT with clients from diverse cultural backgrounds

Format of Class

Classes are 3 hours long. Course time is split evenly between learning DBT theory (lecture/ discussion) and acquiring DBT skills (DBT skills lab):

Lecture/Discussion Class: Each week, there will be one lecture/discussion class for 1.5 hours focusing on DBT theory and related research.

Date	Lecture and Discussion	Skills Lab	Readings
Week 1	Introduction to dialectical behavior therapy (DBT): history, theory, and research; case formulation in DBT	Introduction to principles of deliberate practice	Chapman and Wilks (in press); McMain et al. (2019); Sonley et al. (in press); Swenson (in press)
Week 2	Developing a DBT working alliance; establishing a session agenda	Exercise 1: Establishing a Session Agenda	Boritz et al. (2023); Heard and Swales (2016, Chapter 2); Rizvi (2011)
Week 3	Validation skills	Exercise 2: Validation	Koerner and Linehan (2003); Linehan (1997)
Week 4	Learning principles; reinforcing adaptive behaviors	Exercise 3: Reinforcing Adaptive Behaviors	Chapman (2018); Heard and Swales (2016, Chapter 1)
Week 5	Problem assessment; behavioral chain analysis	Exercise 4: Problem Assessment	Landes (2018, pp. 259–273)
Week 6	Commitment strategies	Exercise 5: Eliciting a Commitment	Pederson (2015, Chapter 15)
Week 7	Midterm paper due, self-evaluation, skill coaching feedback	Exercise 14: Mock sessions (beginner profiles)	No readings
Week 8	Problem solving; solution analysis	Exercise 6: Inviting the Client to Engage in Problem Solving	Heard and Swales (2016, Chapter 4); Landes (2018, pp. 273–282)
Week 9	DBT skills training	Exercise 7: Skills Training	Heard and Swales (2016, Chapter 5); Swales and Dunkley (2020)
Week 10	Modifying cognitions	Exercise 8: Modifying Cognitions	Heard and Swales (2016, Chapter 7)
Week 11	Informal exposure to emotion	Exercise 9: Informal Exposure to Emotions	McMain et al. (2001)
Week 12	Coaching clients in distress	Exercise 10: Coaching Clients in Distress	Linehan and Schmidt (1995)
Week 13	Dialectical strategies	Exercise 11: Promoting Dialectical Thinking Through Both–And Statements	Chapman (2019)
Week 14	Responding to suicidal ideation	Exercise 12: Responding to Suicidal Ideation	Linehan (2016); Mehlum (2018)
Week 15	Final paper due, final exam, self-evaluation, skill coaching feedback	Exercise 14: Mock sessions (intermediate and advanced profiles)	Annotated therapy transcript (Exercise 13)

DBT Skills Lab: Each week there will be one DBT skills lab for 1.5 hours. Skills labs are for practicing DBT skills using the exercises in this book. The exercises use therapy simulations (role-plays) with the following goals:

1. Build trainees' skill and confidence for using DBT skills with real clients
2. Provide a safe space for experimenting with different therapeutic interventions, without fear of making mistakes
3. Provide plenty of opportunity to explore and "try on" different styles of therapy, so trainees can ultimately discover their own personal, unique therapy style

Mock Sessions: Twice in the semester (Weeks 7 and 15), trainees will do a psychotherapy mock session in the DBT skills lab. In contrast to highly structured and repetitive deliberate practice exercises, a psychotherapy mock session is an unstructured and improvised role-played therapy session. Mock sessions allow trainees to

1. practice using DBT skills responsively,
2. experiment with clinical decision making in an unscripted context,
3. discover their personal therapeutic style, and
4. build endurance for working with real clients.

Homework

Homework will be assigned each week and will include reading, 1 hour of skills practice with an assigned practice partner, and occasional writing assignments. For the skills practice homework, trainees will repeat the exercise they did for that week's DBT skills lab. Because the instructor will not be there to evaluate performance, trainees should instead complete the Deliberate Practice Reaction Form, as well as the Deliberate Practice Diary Form, for themselves as a self-evaluation.

Writing Assignments

Students are to write two papers: one due at midterm and one due on the last day of class. The first paper will explore one aspect of DBT theory or the empirical literature on DBT. The second paper will involve the completion of a DBT case formulation and treatment plan.

Multicultural Orientation

Throughout this course, students are encouraged to reflect on their own cultural identity and improve their ability to attune with their clients' cultural identities. In this course, students will be expected to practice within a multicultural orientation that considers cultural safety and cultural humility. For further guidance on this topic and deliberate practice exercises to improve multicultural skills, see the forthcoming book *Deliberate Practice in Multicultural Therapy* (Harris et al., 2022).

Vulnerability, Privacy, and Boundaries

This course is aimed at developing DBT skills (including self-awareness and interpersonal skills) in an experiential framework relevant to clinical work. This course is not psychotherapy or a substitute for psychotherapy: When engaging in role-playing or experiential exercises, students should consider the level of self-disclosure that is appropriate to the context, personally comfortable, and effective for their own learning and that of their classmates. Students are not evaluated on the level of personal material they choose to reveal in the class.

In accordance with the *Ethical Principles of Psychologists and Code of Conduct* (American Psychological Association, 2017), students are **not required to disclose personal information.** Because this class is about developing both interpersonal and DBT competence, following are some important points so that students are fully informed as they make choices to self-disclose:

- Students choose how much, when, and what to disclose. Students are not penalized for the choice not to share personal information.

- The learning environment is susceptible to group dynamics much like any other group space, and therefore students may be asked to share their observations and experiences of the class environment with the singular goal of fostering a more inclusive and productive learning environment.

Confidentiality

To create a safe learning environment that is respectful of client and therapist information and diversity and to foster open and vulnerable conversation in class, students are required to agree to strict confidentiality within and outside of the instruction setting.

Evaluation

Self-Evaluation: At the end of the semester (Week 15), trainees will perform a self-evaluation. This will help trainees track their progress and identify areas for further development. The Guidance for Trainees section in Chapter 3 of *Deliberate Practice in Dialectical Behavior Therapy* highlights potential areas of focus for self-evaluation.

Grading Criteria

Students will be evaluated on the level and quality of their performance in

- the lecture/discussion,
- the skills lab (exercises and mock sessions),
- midterm and final papers, and
- a final exam.

Required Readings

Boritz, T., Varma, S., Sonley, A., & McMain, S. F. (2023). Alliance rupture and repair in dialectical behavior therapy for borderline personality disorder. In C. F. Eubanks, L. W. Samstag, & J. C. Muran (Eds.), *Rupture and repair in psychotherapy: A critical process for change* (pp. 141–164). American Psychological Association. https://doi.org/10.1037/0000306-007

Chapman, A. (2018). Behavioural foundations of DBT: Applying behavioural principles to the challenge of suicidal behaviour and non-suicidal self-injury. In M. Swales (Ed.), *The Oxford handbook of dialectical behavior therapy* (pp. 69–90). Oxford University Press.

Chapman, A. (2019). *Phone coaching in dialectical behavior therapy.* Guilford Press.

Chapman, A., & Wilks, C. (in press). Applications of dialectical behavior therapy. In G. Gabbard (Ed.), *Textbook of psychotherapeutic treatments* (2nd ed.). American Psychiatric Publishing.

Heard, H. L., & Swales, M. A. (2016). *Changing behavior in DBT: Problem solving in action.* Guilford Press.

Koerner, K., & Linehan, M. M. (2003). Validation principles and strategies. In W. O'Donohue, J. E. Fisher, & S. C. Hayes (Eds.), *Cognitive behavioral therapy* (pp. 229–237). John Wiley & Sons, Inc.

Landes, S. (2018). Conducting effective behavioural and solution analyses. In M. Swales (Ed.), *The Oxford handbook of dialectical behavior therapy* (pp. 259–282). Oxford University Press.

Linehan, M. M. (1997). Validation and psychotherapy. In A. C. Bohart & L. S. Greenberg (Eds.), *Empathy reconsidered: New directions in psychotherapy* (pp. 353–392). American Psychological Association.

Linehan, M. M. (2016). Linehan Risk Assessment and Management Protocol (LRAMP). https://depts.washington.edu/uwbrtc/wp-content/uploads/LSSN-LRAMP-v1.0.pdf

Linehan, M. M., & Schmidt, H. III. (1995). The dialectics of effective treatment of borderline personality disorder. In W. O'Donohue & L. Krasner (Eds.), *Theories of behavior therapy: Exploring behavior change* (pp. 553–584). American Psychological Association. https://doi.org/10.1037/10169-020

McMain, S., Korman, L. M., & Dimeff, L. (2001). Dialectical behavior therapy and the treatment of emotion dysregulation. *Journal of Clinical Psychology, 57*(2), 183–196. https://doi.org/10.1002/1097-4679(200102)57:2%3C183::AID-JCLP5%3E3.0.CO;2-Y

McMain, S., Leybman, M., Boritz, T. (2019). Case formulation in dialectical behaviour therapy. In U. Kramer (Ed.). *Case formulation for personality disorders* (pp. 1–18). Academic Press. https://doi.org/10.1016/B978-0-12-813521-1.00001-1

Mehlum, L. (2018). DBT as a suicide and self-harm treatment: Assessing and treating suicidal behaviours. In M. Swales (Ed.), *The Oxford handbook of dialectical behavior therapy* (pp. 307–324). Oxford University Press.

Pederson, L. (2015). *Dialectical behavior therapy: A contemporary guide for practitioners.* Wiley-Blackwell.

Rizvi, S. L. (2011). The therapeutic relationship in dialectical behavior therapy for suicidal individuals. In K. Michel & D. A. Jobes (Eds.), *Building a therapeutic alliance with the suicidal patient* (pp. 255–271). American Psychological Association. https://doi.org/10.1037/12303-014

Sonley, A., Boritz, T., & McMain, S. (in press). Applications of dialectical behavior therapy. In G. Gabbard (Ed.), *Textbook of psychotherapeutic treatments* (2nd ed.). American Psychiatric Publishing.

Swales, M., & Dunkley, C. (2020). Principles of skills assessment in dialectical behavior therapy. *Cognitive and Behavioral Practice, 27*(1), 18–29. https://doi.org/10.1016/j.cbpra.2019.05.001

Swenson, C. (in press). Applications of dialectical behavior therapy. In G. Gabbard (Ed.), *Textbook of psychotherapeutic treatments* (2nd ed.). American Psychiatric Publishing.

Supplemental Readings

Dimeff, L., & Koerner, K. (2007). *Dialectical behavior therapy in clinical practice: Applications across disorders and settings.* Guilford Press.

Koerner, K. (2012). *Doing dialectical behavior therapy: A practical guide.* Guilford Press.

Linehan, M. M. (1993). *Cognitive-behavioral treatment of borderline personality disorder.* Guilford Press.

Linehan, M. M. (2015). *DBT skills training handouts and worksheets* (2nd ed.). Guilford Press.

Linehan, M. M. (2015). *DBT skills training manual* (2nd ed.). Guilford Press.

Linehan, M. M., & Wilks, C. R. (2015). The course and evolution of dialectical behavior therapy. *American Journal of Psychotherapy, 69*(2), 97–110. https://doi.org/10.1176/appi.psychotherapy.2015.69.2.97

Pryor, K. (1999). *Don't shoot the dog: The new art of teaching and training.* Bantam Doubleday Dell Publishing.

Ramnero, J., & Törneke, N. (2008). *The ABCs of human behavior: Behavioral principles for the practicing clinician.* New Harbinger Publications.

Swales, M. (2018). *The Oxford handbook of dialectical behavior therapy.* Oxford University Press.

Swenson, C. R. (2016). *DBT principles in action: Acceptance, change, and dialectics.* Guilford Press.

References

American Psychological Association. (2017). *Ethical principles of psychologists and code of conduct* (2002, Amended June 1, 2010, and January 1, 2017). https://www.apa.org/ethics/code/

Anderson, T., Ogles, B. M., Patterson, C. L., Lambert, M. J., & Vermeersch, D. A. (2009). Therapist effects: Facilitative interpersonal skills as a predictor of therapist success. *Journal of Clinical Psychology*, 65(7), 755–768. https://doi.org/10.1002/jclp.20583

Bailey, R. J., & Ogles, B. M. (2019, August 1). Common factors as a therapeutic approach: What is required? *Practice Innovations*, 4(4), 241–254. https://doi.org/10.1037/pri0000100

Barlow, D. H. (2010). Negative effects from psychological treatments: A perspective. *American Psychologist*, 65(1), 13–20. https://doi.org/10.1037/a0015643

Bedics, J. D., Atkins, D. C., Comtois, K. A., & Linehan, M. M. (2012a). Treatment differences in the therapeutic relationship and introject during a 2-year randomized controlled trial of dialectical behavior therapy versus nonbehavioral psychotherapy experts for borderline personality disorder. *Journal of Consulting and Clinical Psychology*, 80(1), 66–77. https://doi.org/10.1037/a0026113

Bedics, J. D., Atkins, D. C., Comtois, K. A., & Linehan, M. M. (2012b). Weekly therapist ratings of the therapeutic relationship and patient introject during the course of dialectical behavioral therapy for the treatment of borderline personality disorder. *Psychotherapy: Theory, Research, & Practice*, 49(2), 231–240. https://doi.org/10.1037/a0028254

Bedics, J. D., Atkins, D. C., Harned, M. S., & Linehan, M. M. (2015). The therapeutic alliance as a predictor of outcome in dialectical behavior therapy versus nonbehavioral psychotherapy by experts for borderline personality disorder. *Psychotherapy: Theory, Research, & Practice*, 52(1), 67–77. https://doi.org/10.1037/a0038457

Bennett-Levy, J., & Finlay-Jones, A. (2018). The role of personal practice in therapist skill development: A model to guide therapists, educators, supervisors and researchers. *Cognitive Behaviour Therapy*, 47(3), 185–205. https://doi.org/10.1080/16506073.2018.1434678

Bohart, A. C., & Wade, A. G. (2013). The client in psychotherapy. In M. J. Lambert (Ed.), *Bergin and Garfield's handbook of psychotherapy and behavior change* (5th ed., pp. 219–257). John Wiley & Sons.

Boritz, T., Varma, S., Macaulay, C., & McMain, S. F. (2021). Alliance rupture and repair in early sessions of dialectical behavior therapy: The case of Rachel. *Journal of Clinical Psychology*, 77(2), 441–456. https://doi.org/10.1002/jclp.23101

Boritz, T., Varma, S., Sonley, A., & McMain, S. F. (2023). Alliance rupture and repair in dialectical behavior therapy for borderline personality disorder. In C. F. Eubanks, L. W. Samstag, & J. C. Muran (Eds.), *Rupture and repair in psychotherapy: A critical process for change* (pp. 141–164). American Psychological Association. https://doi.org/10.1037/0000306-007

Bugatti, M., & Boswell, J. F. (2016). Clinical errors as a lack of context responsiveness. *Psychotherapy: Theory, Research, & Practice*, 53(3), 262–267. https://doi.org/10.1037/pst0000080

Castonguay, L. G., Goldfried, M. R., Wiser, S., Raue, P. J., & Hayes, A. M. (1996). Predicting the effect of cognitive therapy for depression: A study of unique and common factors. *Journal of Consulting and Clinical Psychology*, 64(3), 497–504. https://doi.org/10.1037/0022-006X.64.3.497

Chapman, A. (2018). Behavioural foundations of DBT: Applying behavioural principles to the challenge of suicidal behaviour and non-suicidal self-injury. In M. Swales (Ed.), *The Oxford handbook of dialectical behavior therapy* (pp. 69–90). Oxford University Press.

Chapman, A. (2019). *Phone coaching in dialectical behavior therapy*. Guilford Press.

Chapman, A., & Wilks, C. (in press). Applications of dialectical behavior therapy. In G. Gabbard (Ed.), *Textbook of psychotherapeutic treatments* (2nd ed.). American Psychiatric Publishing.

Coker, J. (1990). *How to practice jazz*. Jamey Aebersold.

Cook, R. (2005). *It's about that time: Miles Davis on and off record*. Atlantic Books.

Cristea, I. A., Gentili, C., Cotet, C. D., Palomba, D., Barbui, C., & Cuijpers, P. (2017). Efficacy of psychotherapies for borderline personality disorder: A systematic review and meta-analysis. *JAMA Psychiatry*, 74(4), 319–328. https://doi.org/10.1001/jamapsychiatry.2016.4287

Csikszentmihalyi, M. (1997). *Finding flow: The psychology of engagement with everyday life*. Harper Collins.

Dimeff, L. A., Rizvi, S. L., & Koerner, K. (2021). *Dialectical behavior therapy in clinical practice: Applications across disorders and settings*. Guilford Press.

Ellis, M. V., Berger, L., Hanus, A. E., Ayala, E. E., Swords, B. A., & Siembor, M. (2014). Inadequate and harmful clinical supervision: Testing a revised framework and assessing occurrence. *The Counseling Psychologist*, 42(4), 434–472. https://doi.org/10.1177/0011000013508656

Ericsson, K. A. (2003). Development of elite performance and deliberate practice: An update from the perspective of the expert performance approach. In J. L. Starkes & K. A. Ericsson (Eds.), *Expert performance in sports: Advances in research on sport expertise* (pp. 49–81). Human Kinetics.

Ericsson, K. A. (2004). Deliberate practice and the acquisition and maintenance of expert performance in medicine and related domains: Invited address. *Academic Medicine*, 79(10, Suppl.), S70–S81. https://doi.org/10.1097/00001888-200410001-00022

Ericsson, K. A. (2006). The influence of experience and deliberate practice on the development of superior expert performance. In K. A. Ericsson, N. Charness, P. J. Feltovich, & R. R. Hoffman (Eds.), *The Cambridge handbook of expertise and expert performance* (pp. 683–703). Cambridge University Press. https://doi.org/10.1017/CBO9780511816796.038

Ericsson, K. A., Hoffman, R. R., Kozbelt, A., & Williams, A. M. (Eds.). (2018). *The Cambridge handbook of expertise and expert performance* (2nd ed.). Cambridge University Press. https://doi.org/10.1017/9781316480748

Ericsson, K. A., Krampe, R. T., & Tesch-Römer, C. (1993). The role of deliberate practice in the acquisition of expert performance. *Psychological Review*, 100(3), 363–406. https://doi.org/10.1037/0033-295X.100.3.363

Ericsson, K. A., & Pool, R. (2016). *Peak: Secrets from the new science of expertise*. Houghton Mifflin Harcourt.

Fisher, R. P., & Craik, F. I. M. (1977). Interaction between encoding and retrieval operations in cued recall. *Journal of Experimental Psychology: Human Learning and Memory*, 3(6), 701–711. https://doi.org/10.1037/0278-7393.3.6.701

Fruzzetti, A. E., Waltz, J. A., & Linehan, M. M. (1997). Supervision in dialectical behavior therapy. In C. E. Watkins, Jr. (Ed.), *Handbook of psychotherapy supervision* (pp. 84–100). Wiley.

Gladwell, M. (2008). *Outliers: The story of success*. Little, Brown & Company.

Goldberg, S., Rousmaniere, T. G., Miller, S. D., Whipple, J., Nielsen, S. L., Hoyt, W., & Wampold, B. E. (2016). Do psychotherapists improve with time and experience? A longitudinal analysis of outcomes in a clinical setting. *Journal of Counseling Psychology*, 63, 1–11. https://doi.org/10.1037/cou0000131

Goldman, R. N., Vaz, A., & Rousmaniere, T. (2021). *Deliberate practice in emotion-focused therapy*. American Psychological Association. https://doi.org/10.1037/0000227-000

Goodyear, R. K. (2015). Using accountability mechanisms more intentionally: A framework and its implications for training professional psychologists. *American Psychologist*, 70(8), 736–743. https://doi.org/10.1037/a0039828

Goodyear, R. K., & Nelson, M. L. (1997). The major formats of psychotherapy supervision. In C. E. Watkins, Jr. (Ed.), *Handbook of psychotherapy supervision* (pp. 328–344). John Wiley & Sons.

Haggerty, G., & Hilsenroth, M. J. (2011). The use of video in psychotherapy supervision. *British Journal of Psychotherapy*, *27*(2), 193–210. https://doi.org/10.1111/j.1752-0118.2011.01232.x

Harris, J., Jin, J., Hoffman, S., Phan, S., Prout, T. A., Rousmaniere, T., & Vaz, A. (2022). *Deliberate practice in multicultural therapy* [Manuscript in preparation]. American Psychological Association.

Hatcher, R. L. (2015). Interpersonal competencies: Responsiveness, technique, and training in psychotherapy. *American Psychologist*, *70*(8), 747–757. https://doi.org/10.1037/a0039803

Heard, H. L., & Swales, M. A. (2016). *Changing behavior in DBT: Problem solving in action*. Guilford Press.

Henry, W. P., Strupp, H. H., Butler, S. F., Schacht, T. E., & Binder, J. L. (1993). Effects of training in time-limited dynamic psychotherapy: Changes in therapist behavior. *Journal of Consulting and Clinical Psychology*, *61*(3), 434–440. https://doi.org/10.1037/0022-006X.61.3.434

Hill, C. E., Kivlighan, D. M., III, Rousmaniere, T., Kivlighan, D. M., Jr., Gerstenblith, J. A., & Hillman, J. W. (2020). Deliberate practice for the skill of immediacy: A multiple case study of doctoral student therapists and clients. *Psychotherapy*, *57*(4), 587–597. https://doi.org/10.1037/pst0000247

Hill, C. E., & Knox, S. (2013). Training and supervision in psychotherapy: Evidence for effective practice. In M. J. Lambert (Ed.), *Handbook of psychotherapy and behavior change* (6th ed., pp. 775–811). John Wiley & Sons.

Kendall, P. C., & Beidas, R. S. (2007). Smoothing the trail for dissemination of evidence-based practices for youth: Flexibility within fidelity. *Professional Psychology, Research and Practice*, *38*(1), 13–19. https://doi.org/10.1037/0735-7028.38.1.13

Kendall, P. C., & Frank, H. E. (2018). Implementing evidence-based treatment protocols: Flexibility within fidelity. *Clinical Psychology: Science and Practice*, *25*(4), e12271. https://doi.org/10.1111/cpsp.12271

Koerner, K., & Linehan, M. M. (2003). Validation principles and strategies. In W. O'Donohue, J. E. Fisher, & S. C. Hayes (Eds.), *Cognitive behavioral therapy* (pp. 229–237). John Wiley & Sons, Inc.

Koziol, L. F., & Budding, D. E. (2012). Procedural learning. In N. M. Seel (Ed.), *Encyclopedia of the sciences of learning* (pp. 2694–2696). Springer. https://doi.org/10.1007/978-1-4419-1428-6_670

Lambert, M. J. (2010). Yes, it is time for clinicians to monitor treatment outcome. In B. L. Duncan, S. C. Miller, B. E. Wampold, & M. A. Hubble (Eds.), *Heart and soul of change: Delivering what works in therapy* (2nd ed., pp. 239–266). American Psychological Association. https://doi.org/10.1037/12075-008

Landes, S. (2018). Conducting effective behavioural and solution analyses. In M. Swales (Ed.), *The Oxford handbook of dialectical behavior therapy* (pp. 259–282). Oxford University Press.

Linehan, M. (1993a). *Cognitive-behavioral treatment of borderline personality disorder*. Guilford Press.

Linehan, M. M. (1993b). *Skills training manual for treating borderline personality disorder*. Guilford Press.

Linehan, M. M. (1997). Validation and psychotherapy. In A. C. Bohart & L. S. Greenberg (Eds.), *Empathy reconsidered: New directions in psychotherapy* (pp. 353–392). American Psychological Association.

Linehan, M. M. (2016). Linehan Risk Assessment and Management Protocol (LRAMP). https://depts.washington.edu/uwbrtc/wp-content/uploads/LSSN-LRAMP-v1.0.pdf

Linehan, M. M., & Schmidt, H. III. (1995). The dialectics of effective treatment of borderline personality disorder. In W. O'Donohue & L. Krasner (Eds.), *Theories of behavior therapy: Exploring behavior change* (pp. 553–584). American Psychological Association. https://doi.org/10.1037/10169-020

Markman, K. D., & Tetlock, P. E. (2000). Accountability and close-call counterfactuals: The loser who nearly won and the winner who nearly lost. *Personality and Social Psychology Bulletin*, *26*(10), 1213–1224. https://doi.org/10.1177/0146167200262004

McGaghie, W. C., Issenberg, S. B., Barsuk, J. H., & Wayne, D. B. (2014). A critical review of simulation-based mastery learning with translational outcomes. *Medical Education, 48*(4), 375–385. https://doi.org/10.1111/medu.12391

McLeod, J. (2017). Qualitative methods for routine outcome measurement. In T. G. Rousmaniere, R. Goodyear, D. D. Miller, & B. E. Wampold (Eds.), *The cycle of excellence: Using deliberate practice to improve supervision and training* (pp. 99–122). John Wiley & Sons. https://doi.org/10.1002/9781119165590.ch5

McMain, S., Korman, L. M., & Dimeff, L. (2001). Dialectical behavior therapy and the treatment of emotion dysregulation. *Journal of Clinical Psychology, 57*(2), 183–196. https://doi.org/10.1002/1097-4679(200102)57:2%3C183::AID-JCLP5%3E3.0.CO;2-Y

McMain, S., Leybman, M., & Boritz, T. (2019). Case formulation in dialectical behaviour therapy. In U. Kramer (Ed.), *Case formulation for personality disorders* (pp. 1–18). Academic Press. https://doi.org/10.1016/B978-0-12-813521-1.00001-1

McMain, S., & Wiebe, C. (2013). *Dialectical behavior therapy for emotion dysregulation* [Video]. Psychotherapy.net.

Mehlum, L. (2018). DBT as a suicide and self-harm treatment: Assessing and treating suicidal behaviours. In M. Swales (Ed.), *The Oxford handbook of dialectical behavior therapy* (pp. 307–324). Oxford University Press.

Norcross, J. C., & Guy, J. D. (2005). The prevalence and parameters of personal therapy in the United States. In J. D. Geller, J. C. Norcross, & D. E. Orlinsky (Eds.), *The psychotherapist's own psychotherapy: Patient and clinician perspectives* (pp. 165–176). Oxford University Press.

Norcross, J. C., Lambert, M. J., & Wampold, B. E. (2019). *Psychotherapy relationships that work* (3rd ed.). Oxford University Press.

Orlinsky, D. E., Rønnestad, M. H., & Collaborative Research Network of the Society for Psychotherapy Research. (2005). *How psychotherapists develop: A study of therapeutic work and professional growth.* American Psychological Association. https://doi.org/10.1037/11157-000

Owen, J., & Hilsenroth, M. J. (2014). Treatment adherence: The importance of therapist flexibility in relation to therapy outcomes. *Journal of Counseling Psychology, 61*(2), 280-288. https://doi.org/10.1037/a0035753

Pederson, L. (2015). *Dialectical behavior therapy: A contemporary guide for practitioners.* Wiley-Blackwell.

Prescott, D. S., Maeschalck, C. L., & Miller, S. D. (2017). *Feedback-informed treatment in clinical practice: Reaching for excellence.* American Psychological Association. https://doi.org/10.1037/0000039-000

Rizvi, S. L. (2011). The therapeutic relationship in dialectical behavior therapy for suicidal individuals. In K. Michel & D. A. Jobes (Eds.), *Building a therapeutic alliance with the suicidal patient* (pp. 255–271). American Psychological Association. https://doi.org/10.1037/12303-014

Rousmaniere, T. G. (2016). *Deliberate practice for psychotherapists: A guide to improving clinical effectiveness.* Routledge Press/Taylor & Francis. https://doi.org/10.4324/9781315472256

Rousmaniere, T. G. (2019). *Mastering the inner skills of psychotherapy: A deliberate practice handbook.* Gold Lantern Press.

Rousmaniere, T. G., Goodyear, R., Miller, S. D., & Wampold, B. E. (Eds.). (2017). *The cycle of excellence: Using deliberate practice to improve supervision and training.* Wiley Publishers. https://doi.org/10.1002/9781119165590

Sayrs, J. H. R., & Linehan, M. M. (2019). *DBT teams: Development and practice.* Guilford Press.

Shearin, E. N., & Linehan, M. M. (1992). Patient–therapist ratings and relationship to progress in dialectical behavior therapy for borderline personality disorder. *Behavior Therapy, 23*(4), 730–741. https://doi.org/10.1016/S0005-7894(05)80232-1

Shneidman, E. S. (1992). A conspectus of the suicidal scenario. In R. W. Maris, A. L. Berman, J. T. Maltsberger, & R. I. Yufit (Eds.), *Assessment and prediction of suicide* (pp. 50–64). Guilford Press.

Sonley, A., Boritz, T., & McMain, S. (in press). Applications of dialectical behavior therapy. In G. Gabbard (Ed.), *Textbook of psychotherapeutic treatments* (2nd ed.). American Psychiatric Publishing.

Squire, L. R. (2004). Memory systems of the brain: A brief history and current perspective. *Neurobiology of Learning and Memory, 82*(3), 171–177. https://doi.org/10.1016/j.nlm.2004.06.005

Stiles, W. B., Honos-Webb, L., & Surko, M. (1998). Responsiveness in psychotherapy. *Clinical Psychology: Science and Practice, 5*(4), 439–458. https://doi.org/10.1111/j.1468-2850.1998.tb00166.x

Stiles, W. B., & Horvath, A. O. (2017). Appropriate responsiveness as a contribution to therapist effects. In L. G. Castonguay & C. E. Hill (Eds.), *How and why are some therapists better than others? Understanding therapist effects* (pp. 71–84). American Psychological Association. https://doi.org/10.1037/0000034-005

Stoffers, J. M., Völlm, B. A., Rücker, G., Timmer, A., Huband, N., & Lieb, K. (2012). Psychological therapies for people with borderline personality disorder. *The Cochrane Database of Systematic Reviews, 2012*(8), CD005652.

Storebø, O. J., Stoffers-Winterling, J. M., Völlm, B. A., Kongerslev, M. T., Mattivi, J. T., Jørgensen, M. S., Faltinsen, E., Todorovac, A., Sales, C. P., Callesen, H. E., Lieb, K., & Simonsen, E. (2020). Psychological therapies for people with borderline personality disorder. *Cochrane Database of Systematic Reviews, 5*(5), CD012955.

Swales, M., & Dunkley, C. (2020). Principles of skills assessment in dialectical behavior therapy. *Cognitive and Behavioral Practice, 27*(1), 18–29. https://doi.org/10.1016/j.cbpra.2019.05.001

Swenson, C. (in press). Applications of dialectical behavior therapy. In G. Gabbard (Ed.), *Textbook of psychotherapeutic treatments* (2nd ed.). American Psychiatric Publishing.

Taylor, J. M., & Neimeyer, G. J. (2017). Lifelong professional improvement: The evolution of continuing education. In T. G. Rousmaniere, R. Goodyear, S. D. Miller, & B. Wampold (Eds.), *The cycle of excellence: Using deliberate practice to improve supervision and training* (pp. 219–248). John Wiley & Sons.

Tracey, T. J. G., Wampold, B. E., Goodyear, R. K., & Lichtenberg, J. W. (2015). Improving expertise in psychotherapy. *Psychotherapy Bulletin, 50*(1), 7–13.

Tullos, J. M. (Director & Producer), & Governors State University, Division of Digital Learning and Media Design (Producer). (2014). *Dialectical behavior therapy* [Video/DVD]. American Psychological Association. https://video.alexanderstreet.com/watch/dialectical-behavior-therapy-2

Waltz, J. L., Fruzzetti, A. E., & Linehan, M. M. (1998). The role of supervision in dialectical behavior therapy. *The Clinical Supervisor, 17*(1), 101–113. https://doi.org/10.1300/J001v17n01_09

Wass, R., & Golding, C. (2014). Sharpening a tool for teaching: The zone of proximal development. *Teaching in Higher Education, 19*(6), 671–684. https://doi.org/10.1080/13562517.2014.901958

Yalom, V., Yalom, M.-H., Sharp, B., Grashuis, H., Linehan, M., & Read, K. (2013). *3 approaches to personality disorders: 3-Video series.* Psychotherapy.net.

Zaretskii, V. (2009). The zone of proximal development: What Vygotsky did not have time to write. *Journal of Russian & East European Psychology, 47*(6), 70–93. https://doi.org/10.2753/RPO1061-0405470604

Index

About the Authors

Tali Boritz, PhD, CPsych, is an assistant professor in the Department of Psychology at York University and a collaborator scientist at the Centre for Addiction and Mental Health in Toronto, Ontario, Canada. She is a registered clinical psychologist and specializes in dialectical behavior therapy (DBT) with individuals with borderline personality disorder (BPD). She regularly conducts DBT training workshops and is involved in numerous initiatives related to the enhancement of psychotherapy training. She has published extensively on DBT, BPD, and psychotherapy process and outcome research. Dr. Boritz is currently president-elect of the North American Society for Psychotherapy Research.

Shelley McMain, PhD, CPsych, is the head of the Borderline Personality Disorder Clinic and a clinician scientist at the Centre for Addiction and Mental Health in Toronto, Ontario, Canada. She is the director of the Psychotherapy, Humanities and Psychosocial Intervention Division and an associate professor in the Department of Psychiatry at the University of Toronto. She is a certified dialectical behavior therapy (DBT) individual and group therapist. She currently serves as the president of the International Society for Psychotherapy Research as well as the acting president of the World DBT Association. Dr. McMain has authored several papers on DBT and coauthored a book with instructional video on DBT (*Psychotherapy Essentials to Go: Dialectical Behavior Therapy for Emotion Dysregulation*, 2013). She has delivered more than 300 conference presentations, colloquia, grand rounds, and trainings. She is widely recognized for her excellence in DBT training. She has received several international awards for her psychotherapy research (e.g., European Society for the Study of Personality Disorders, American Psychoanalytic Society) and various teaching awards.

Alexandre Vaz, PhD, is cofounder and chief academic officer of Sentio University, Los Angeles, California. He provides deliberate practice workshops and advanced clinical training and supervision to clinicians around the world. Dr. Vaz is the author/coeditor of multiple books on deliberate practice and psychotherapy training and two series of clinical training books: The Essentials of Deliberate Practice (American Psychological Association) and Advanced Therapeutics, Clinical and Interpersonal Skills (Elsevier). He has held multiple committee roles for the Society for the Exploration of Psychotherapy Integration and the Society for Psychotherapy Research. Dr. Vaz is founder and host of "Psychotherapy Expert Talks," an acclaimed interview series with distinguished psychotherapists and therapy researchers.

Tony Rousmaniere, PsyD, is cofounder and program director of Sentio University, Los Angeles, California. He provides workshops, webinars, and advanced clinical training and supervision to clinicians around the world. Dr. Rousmaniere is the author/coeditor of multiple books on deliberate practice and psychotherapy training and two series of clinical training books: The Essentials of Deliberate Practice (American Psychological Association) and Advanced Therapeutics, Clinical and Interpersonal Skills (Elsevier). In 2017, he published the widely cited article "What Your Therapist Doesn't Know," in *The Atlantic Monthly*. He supports the open-data movement and publishes his aggregated clinical outcome data, in deidentified form, on his website (https://drtonyr.com/). A Fellow of the American Psychological Association, Dr. Rousmaniere was awarded the Early Career Award by the Society for the Advancement of Psychotherapy (APA Division 29).